Lifeguard Training Activities and Games

Lifeguard Training Activities and Games

Susan J. Grosse, MS

Human Kinetics

Library of Congress Cataloging-in-Publication Data

Grosse, Susan J., 1946-
    Lifeguard training activities and games / Susan J. Grosse.
      p. cm.
    ISBN-13: 978-0-7360-7929-7 (soft cover)
    ISBN-10: 0-7360-7929-7 (soft cover)
  1. Lifeguards--Training of.   I. Title.
    GV838.74.G76   2009
    797.2'00289--dc22

2009001398

ISBN-10: 0-7360-7929-7 (print)   ISBN-10: 0-7360-8671-4 (Adobe PDF)
ISBN-13: 978-0-7360-7929-7 (print)   ISBN-13: 978-0-7360-8671-4 (Adobe PDF)

Copyright © 2009 by Susan J. Grosse

The Web addresses cite[...] lerwise noted.

Acquisitions Editor: [...] **Assistant Editor:** Anne Rumery; **Copyeditor:** [...] **Permission Manager:** Martha Gullo; **Graphic** [...] dberg; **Cover Designer:** Robert Reuther; **Photo**[...] **Production Manager:** Jason Allen; **Art Man**[...] **Manager:** Alan L. Wilborn; **Printer:** Versa Press

We thank the F.J. Gaenslen School in Milwaukee, Wisconsin, for assistance in providing the location for the photo shoot for this book.

Printed in the United States of America   10 9 8 7 6 5 4 3 2 1

The paper in this book is certified under a sustainable forestry program.

Human Kinetics
Web site: www.HumanKinetics.com

United States: Human Kinetics
P.O. Box 5076
Champaign, IL 61825-5076
800-747-4457
e-mail: humank@hkusa.com

Canada: Human Kinetics
475 Devonshire Road Unit 100
Windsor, ON N8Y 2L5
800-465-7301 (in Canada only)
e-mail: info@hkcanada.com

Europe: Human Kinetics
107 Bradford Road
Stanningley
Leeds LS28 6AT, United Kingdom
+44 (0) 113 255 5665
e-mail: hk@hkeurope.com

Australia: Human Kinetics
57A Price Avenue
Lower Mitcham, South Australia 5062
08 8372 0999
e-mail: info@hkaustralia.com

New Zealand: Human Kinetics
Division of Sports Distributors NZ Ltd.
P.O. Box 300 226 Albany
North Shore City
Auckland
0064 9 448 1207
e-mail: info@humankinetics.co.nz

Contents

Activity Finder

CONDITIONING ACTIVITIES

Activity name	Page number	Cardio	Strength	Endurance	Flexibility
Aqua Square Dance	194	X		X	X
Aqua Step	201	X	X	X	X
Arm Tread	21	X	X	X	
Avoid It	22	X	X	X	
Board or Bar Push	23		X	X	
Bottom Tag	94	X		X	
Bounce-Ups	25		X	X	
Brick Pass	26		X	X	
Brick-Ups	27	X	X	X	X
Brick-Ups R & Rs	28	X		X	
Buoy Ball Transport	178		X		
Cage Ball Pass	29			X	X
Cancan Line	179	X		X	
Clean the Pool	95	X		X	X
Clothes Caper	30	X	X		X
Clothesline Relay	31	X	X	X	X
Clothes Swim	33	X	X	X	X
Clothing Flotation	34	X		X	X
Clothing Scramble	35	X		X	X
Craft by Hand	36		X		X
Endurance CPR	146	X		X	
Fitness Testing	209	X	X	X	
Follow the Leader	37	X	X	X	X
Group 500-Yard Swim	38	X	X	X	
Hand Jive	39	X	X	X	
Holiday Celebrations	211	X		X	X
Hydro Uno	41	X		X	
Jammer Catch	42	X		X	
Journaling	216	X	X	X	X
Keep It Up!	43	X		X	
Kickboard Scoot	44	X	X	X	
Lap Chase Tag	45	X		X	
Leapfrog	102	X		X	X
Lifeguard Competitions	223	X	X	X	X
Musical Bricks	46	X	X	X	
Musical Tubes	47	X	X	X	X
Paddle, Swim, Paddle	123	X		X	
Pass It On	48			X	X
PFD Swap	49			X	X
Polka Jog	224	X	X	X	X
Poly Trail	50	X		X	X
Push Me Pull You	51	X	X	X	X
Relays	228	X	X	X	X
Rescue Board Maze	107	X	X		X
Rescue Board Pull-Ups	108		X		
Rescue Board Push-Ups	184		X		
Rescue Board Slalom	124	X	X		X
Rescue Tube Challenge	110	X	X	X	
Rescue Tube Tug-of-War	111		X	X	
Scoop Ball Catch	52	X		X	
Scoop Ball Pass Around	53	X		X	X

...continued

CONTITIONING ACTIVITIES ...continued

SAFETY, SURVEILLANCE, AND SCANNING ACTIVITIES

Activity name	Page number	Safety awareness	Safety skills	Scanning	Surveillance
Accident Reports	135	X			
Bloody Gloves	139	X	X		
Challenge Testing	204		X		
Clothes Swim	33	X	X		
Clothing Flotation	34	X	X		
Color Scan	70			X	X
CPR by Touch	140	X	X		
Craft by Hand	36	X	X		
Cross Bearings	96		X		
Disaster Drill	144	X	X		
Drippy Mani CPR	145		X		
Endurance CPR	146	X	X		
Everyone's a Swimmer	97	X	X		
Extend Your Reach	99	X	X		
Field Experiences	207	X	X		
Flash Card Victims	71				X
Guard Arrangement	73			X	X
It's YOUR Job	180	X			
Jeopardy	147	X			
Job Trade	182	X			
Junior Guard Activities	218	X	X		
Lifeguard Competitions	223	X	X	X	X
Locate and Retrieve	74				X
Missing Task	148		X		
No Space	150	X	X		
Pass the Message	75			X	X
PFD Swap	49	X	X		
Pool Design	76	X			
Poster Design	77	X			
Ring Buoy Repeats	125		X		
Safety Check	78	X			
Safety Concentration	80	X			
Safety Day	82	X	X		
Scan Test	83			X	X
Scrambled Response	155	X	X		
Scrambled Sequences	84		X		
Shake Out	186		X		
Surviving the Challenge	116	X	X		
Teach One	86	X	X		
Unusual Circumstance Debriefing	166	X			
Video Evaluation	171	X			
What's My Zone?	88			X	X
What Went Wrong?	172	X	X		
Zone Art	89			X	X

AQUATIC RESCUE SKILL ACTIVITIES

Activity name	Page number	Coordination	Swim skills or treading	Equipment handling	Rescue skills
Rescue Board Slalom	124			X	
Rescue Maze	109	X		X	X
Rescue Relay	185			X	X
Rescue Tube Challenge	110		X	X	
Rescue Tube Tug-of-War	111			X	
Ring Buoy Repeats	125			X	X
Scavenger Hunt	112		X	X	
Scoop Ball Catch	52		X		
Scoop Ball Pass Around	53		X		
Scrambled Response	155				X
Shake Out	186			X	
Shark's Teeth	113		X		
Shooter Shoot	54		X		
Simon Says	55		X		
Sinker	114	X	X		X
Slip 'n Slide CPR	157			X	X
Speed Shuttle	115	X	X		X
Spontaneous Discovery	158				X
Surprise	159				X
Surviving the Challenge	116		X		X
Swim and Reverse	118	X	X	X	X
Swim the World	56		X		
Teach One	86			X	X
Team Parachute	187	X	X		
Team Surf	126			X	
Timed Events	229	X	X		
Tippy Board	119			X	
Towel Swim	57		X		
Travel Tread	58	X	X	X	
Tube Shift	127			X	X
Tube Sit Race	59	X		X	
Two on a Tube Tug	61	X		X	
Victims, Victims, Victims	169			X	X
Volley	62		X		
Water Polo	64		X		
Weighted Tread	66		X		

CPR, EMERGENCY RESPONSE, AND RISK MANAGEMENT ACTIVITIES

Activity name	Page number	Risk management	Emergency response	CPR	First aid
Accident Reports	135	X	X		
Bloody Gloves	139	X	X	X	X
Challenge Testing	204	X	X	X	X
CPR by Touch	140	X	X	X	
Debriefing	141	X	X		
Disaster Drill	144	X	X		X
Drippy Mani CPR	145		X	X	
Endurance CPR	146		X	X	
Everyone's a Swimmer	97	X	X		
Field Experiences	207	X	X		
Flash Card Victims	71		X	X	X
Guard Arrangement	73	X			
It's YOUR Job	180	X	X		
Jeopardy	147	X	X	X	X
Job Trade	182	X			
Journaling	216	X	X		
Junior Guard Activities	218	X			
Lifeguard Competitions	223		X	X	X
Locate and Retrieve	74		X		
Missing Task	148	X	X	X	X
Multiple-Injury Victim	149		X	X	X
No Space	150		X	X	X
Pool Design	76	X			
Poster Design	77	X			
Pot Luck	151		X	X	X
Q & A	152		X	X	X
Rescue Relay	185		X		
Role Play Debriefing	153	X	X		
Safety Check	78	X			
Safety Concentration	80	X		X	X
Safety Day	82	X			
Scrambled Response	155		X		
Scrambled Sequences	84		X	X	X
Slip 'n Slide CPR	157		X	X	
Spontaneous Discovery	158	X	X		
Surprise	159	X	X		
Surviving the Challenge	116	X	X	X	X
Teach One	86			X	X
Theater World	161	X	X		
Timed Events	229		X		
Two-on-One Pulse Check	162			X	X
Unpredictable Challenge	164		X	X	X
Unusual Circumstance Debriefing	166	X	X		
Victims, Victims, Victims	169	X	X	X	X
Video Evaluation	171	X	X		
What Went Wrong?	172	X	X		

TEAM-BUILDING ACTIVITIES

Activity name	Page number	Partner activities	Team activities
Aqua Square Dance	194	X	
Blind Slalom	120	X	
Buoy Ball Transport	178	X	X
Cancan Line	179		X
Craft by Hand	36	X	X
Cross Bearings	96		X
Extend Your Reach	99		X
Find the Flag	122		X
Four-Man Tube Relay	100		X
Group 500-Yard Swim	38		X
Hand Jive	39	X	
Holiday Celebrations	211	X	X
It's YOUR Job	180		X
Job Trade	182	X	X
Junior Guard Activities	218		X
Keep It Up!	43	X	X
Knots	183		X
Lifeguard Competitions	223		X
Relays	228	X	X
Rescue Board Push-Ups	184	X	X
Rescue Relay	185		X
Shake Out	186	X	X
Team Parachute	187		X
Team Surf	126	X	X
Timed Events	229	X	X
Two on a Tube Tug	61	X	
Victims, Victims, Victims	169		X
Water Polo	64	X	X

Foreword

As instructors and instructor trainers, we have all conducted training sessions with the belief that we are providing lifeguards with the opportunities to learn and improve their knowledge and skills. Throughout my career, I have seen in-service training sessions that were very intense, where it was almost "survival of the fittest." Others have been no more than social gatherings where information may or may not have been exchanged.

I have heard in-service training referred to as:

- Maintaining knowledge and skills at the appropriate level
- Requiring lifeguards to practice every skill every possible way it may happen
- Reinforcing skills through practice with corrective feedback

We all have our own specialties—the subjects, skills, and drills that we have learned and developed over the years. But what new ideas have we embraced that allow us to develop better lifeguards? Maybe even better lifeguards than we are today!

I was once asked this question as a student in physical education: What do you want to have at the end of 15 years of teaching—one year of experience repeated 15 times or 15 years of experience? Ask yourself what you have added or changed in your training program that has made it improve.

In her book *Lifeguard Training Activities and Games*, Sue Grosse provides us with activities that use all of the learning methods: tactile, visual, and auditory. Many of the activities not only show lifeguards *how* to do the skill but also *why* it is done that way. She promotes teamwork through traditional and nontraditional drills and activities. She teaches us to think outside of the box. It doesn't always have to be done the same way.

Over the years, lifeguard training organizations have improved their sessions on surveillance and scanning. The variations of drills and activities in this book now allow us to expand even further on those fundamentals.

Recognition of and reaction to emergencies have been important parts of all lifeguard training programs. Chapter 5 (CPR, Emergency Response, and Risk Management Activities) expands on that information and encourages us not only to react but to remember: What happened, how did it happen, what did we do in response? And how do we improve? These are now areas that help us prepare lifeguards for possible litigation.

The emphasis now is on developing the overall person as well as just a lifeguard. Some nontraditional activities deal with empowerment, communication skills, and language arts. To be a good instructor, you need to do four things:

1. Plan ahead.
2. Be organized.
3. Explain and demonstrate clearly.
4. Involve everyone in every drill and skill.

This book provides us with a variety of learning opportunities. It emphasizes learning, but provides opportunities for learning to be fun. This book should be in the library of anyone who is responsible for the training and development of lifeguards.

Tom Werts
President of Aquatic Safety Consulting

Preface

Certification is only the first step in the ongoing process of training a lifeguard to be a proficient member of a high functioning emergency response team. Training must continue on the job, and the implementation of that training is the responsibility of the aquatic manager or lifeguard supervisor. *Lifeguard Training Activities and Games* is a complete resource for people who are responsible for conducting site-specific on-the-job training for lifeguards. This compilation of aquatic fitness activities, skill drills, team-building events, and games is designed to enhance training and conditioning of lifeguards. Members of the training staff can use this book for guidance as they work to create a highly effective staff of lifeguards.

This book provides over 70 proven training activities and games. The activities are divided into chapters based on various categories of lifeguarding skills. Each activity is short enough to be part of an in-service or class warm-up session. Most activities have variations, allowing for continued challenges as participants move through increasing levels of difficulty. Chapter 1 discusses how, from the entry-level guard to the seasoned veteran, lifeguards can use these activities not only to keep personal performance at a high level, but also continue to meet recertification requirements.

The activities and games in chapter 2 emphasize the development of physical fitness specific to aquatic performance, including endurance, strength, flexibility, and cardiorespiratory function. Lap swimming, the most common method of lifeguard conditioning, can be boring and tedious. By varying the conditioning activities used, you can increase interest and break monotony for your participants. The conditioning activities in this chapter are based on essential lifeguard skills. Therefore, skill learning is enhanced while physical fitness is developed. Keeping fun and challenge in the training process increases enjoyment and fosters participation.

The activities and games in chapters 3 through 5 emphasize lifeguard surveillance, emergency response, and rescue skills. These activities include the use of standard rescue equipment—including rescue tubes, rescue boards, masks, fins, and snorkels—as well as unique equipment such as space shooters and Spin Jammers. Individual challenge and self-testing activities, partner challenges, and team competitions are all represented.

Teamwork is one of the most important components of lifeguard response during an emergency, but it is often overlooked in training programs. Chapter 6 provides fun and interesting problem-solving activities to get any group of individuals working together as a team. Chapter 7 explores how to use special events or longer activities as unique training and team-building opportunities.

All of the activities presented will enhance lifeguard capabilities no matter what type or level of national certification the lifeguard holds. A variety of programs are available for the training and certification of lifeguards, each with specific certification criteria. *Lifeguard Training Activities and Games* supports all of these programs, without particular program bias. This book is a comprehensive resource providing you with a surplus of creative ideas for the ongoing training of your lifeguards. These ideas will help you keep your lifeguards at maximum readiness from the moment they join your staff.

Acknowledgments

Before the production of this book, I wrote and published two publications titled *Lifeguard Training Games and Gimmicks*. These publications were about having fun, and they were also about the serious and hard work leading to the accomplishment of certification in lifeguarding. They were dedicated to people who exemplify the application of these concepts.

On the first day of teaching my very first lifesaving class, I was dismayed when I saw a teenager come into the class on crutches (she was a polio survivor). My supervisor told me, "No problem; she can do it." To Beverly Mills, Julian Stein, and Louise Priest, I give my heartfelt thanks for teaching me that accomplishment is possible for everyone. Yes, the young lady did do it and did it very well.

No matter how difficult the work and how serious the endeavor, fun lightens the load and is a necessary component of learning. Sandra VanAble, Ginny Reister, Ann Wieser, Ruth Sova, and Gail Evans had a tough job—teaching me how to play. I am so glad they persevered in the attempt. Having fun (along with reaping the benefits of accomplishment) brings quality to purpose.

For making sure I never became complacent, or content in my niche, I thank Donna Wetzel, who taught me there were lots of things I had never done before—things that I was perfectly capable of doing if I was willing to try. With the support of colleagues, mentors, and friends, I found that trying eventually became second nature.

No one succeeds in isolation. Most important to my work on this book were all of my students and colleagues who participated in the activities recounted here. I deeply appreciate the efforts of all of these individuals. They took whatever I proposed (maybe demanded?) and were willing to try—even in the coldest of water and during the longest of sessions. They accomplished wonders and had fun while engaging in the very serious and difficult process of becoming knowledgeable and competent lifeguards.

This text contains material provided by other lifeguarding instructors. To Tia Fizzano, Carrie Paterson, Sue Skaros, and Ann Wieser, I express my gratitude for their willingness to share their own fun and challenging activities. Sharing is the key to the survival of any successful aquatic program. Sharing takes a good idea and multiplies it by all of those who take that idea and make it their own, creating a wealth of content in our discipline.

Last but not least, I want to mention that all of the photos in this text were shot at F.J. Gaenslen School, part of the Milwaukee Public School System. I am grateful for access to this fine facility, as well as for our lifeguard models, employees of the Milwaukee Public Schools Division of Municipal Recreation and

Community Services, under the supervision of Nicole Jacobson. Our lifeguard photo models included Thandi Ganya, Autumn Milanowski, Yaphet Morales, Erica Lee Moschetz, William Reynolds, Denzel Shareef, and Jamahl Turner.

Lifeguarding instructors Nicole Jacobson (MPS Division of Recreation and Community Services), Carrie Paterson (F.J. Gaenslen School), and Sue Skaros (Medical College of Wisconsin) led many of the activities. Swimmer volunteers Nick Mike and Jordan Paterson ably assisted them by being willing victims and swimming in group activities. My heartfelt appreciation to one and all.

Developing a High-Performance Staff Through Training Activities and Games

1

National-level programs in lifeguard training and certification provide a sound foundation for lifeguards. But they are just that—a beginning. It is up to the aquatic manager or lifeguard supervisor to take that newly certified lifeguard and help him develop into a highly skilled professional rescuer. The manager or supervisor must also provide opportunities for all staff members to maintain a high level of physical fitness and response capability. Games, skill drills, challenge activities, and self-testing exercises can be used in meeting this need.

Leadership activities help people develop responsibility and pride in achievement. Lifeguards need to be role models for younger program participants, demonstrating behaviors that promote safe participation in aquatic activities. The activities and games in this book contribute to leadership development not only by emphasizing the quality of performance but also by stressing a professional attitude. Lifeguards are trained to function alongside experienced professionals in safety and emergency response situations. The activities in this book can be used to provide training that continues where national training programs leave off in the development of competent lifeguards. This includes (but is not limited to) the promotion of physical conditioning, the development of knowledge and skills in emergency response and rescue, the facilitation of risk management, and the implementation of aquatic leadership training.

Why Activities and Games?

Lifeguarding is serious business. Having knowledge and skills in the area of emergency response is extremely valuable. Using those capabilities to save a life is priceless. When a person is placed in a leadership position that depends on that knowledge and capability, this is recognition not only of hours of training but also of personal characteristics such as judgment, responsibility, and compassion. Lifeguarding is not a game! Training to become a lifeguard and to maintain that certification is equally serious.

But being highly involved in such a serious endeavor can have drawbacks. Making the transition from swimmer to guard might be easy for some. However, because this transition often comes during a person's teenage years (which are already tumultuous), many prospective lifeguards fail to develop the self-discipline necessary for mastering the required skills. Even experienced guards—who are aware of the need for ongoing physical conditioning, practice of rescue skills, and reinforcement of necessary knowledge—might become bored with repetitive drills. It is easy to develop a reliance on what has been done in the past. Lifeguard program leaders and aquatic managers need to establish an atmosphere where staff members have ongoing opportunities for training that is unique and continually challenging. Activities and games can enhance a variety of areas within a lifeguard program.

Development of cognitive skills and abilities relies, for the most part, on book learning and memorization. However, for some people who would make good lifeguards—responsible and mature individuals who are strong swimmers—learning from printed material is very difficult. For these people, activities and games provide reinforcement of text material as well as direct application of text content.

Lifeguard training is more than what happens in the classroom and pool during each class session. It is broader than certification requirements. Lifeguarding is more than being at a station six hours a day and watching people swim. Maintaining high standards in any lifeguarding program requires more than recertification testing. A total lifeguard program should have training components, conditioning, rescue simulations, special activities to enhance training, and field experiences. Participants should move through progressions in developing and maintaining knowledge and skills. A complete lifeguard program includes ongoing preparation for the physical, mental, and psychological challenges that may be faced in the future.

For any lifeguard program to succeed, the aquatic manager must find a way to link the serious business of emergency response (and the study and training required to be able to make that response) to the needs and desires of young people. Jean Twenge, discussing what she terms Generation Me, characterizes today's young adults—including those of lifeguard age (age 16 through their 20s)—as individuals who have been raised receiving praise, good grades, and other rewards that were given to help them develop self-esteem and self-love (Twenge, 2006). This is in direct contrast to receiving praise, good grades, and other rewards because they have been earned—through hard work, meeting established criteria, or performing up to set standards. Feeling good about oneself is now a more popular goal than actual achievement, skill development, and knowledge acquisition. A definite gap exists between the characteristics of Generation Me and the characteristics necessary for commitment to the tasks of being a lifeguard. How does an aquatic manager bridge this gap? Activities and games can forge links to bridge that gap. Through activities and games, lifeguards can do the following:

- Build self-esteem through successful and skilled participation

- Develop teamwork skills through group experiences (noncompetitive as well as competitive)

- Establish a feeling of personal security through belonging to a group of individuals with similar abilities, skills, and commitment

- Learn that hard work and actual achievement can result in consequences of greater value than rewards given for effort and self-esteem

- Enjoy developing knowledge and skills that will serve them well through-out their entire lives
- Have fun in the pursuit of greater personal accomplishment
- Become leaders through a clearly defined process of skill and knowledge development

Not only can a member of Generation Me become an effective lifeguard, she can also continue on to become an aquatic leader.

At some point, all lifeguards must recertify. Ideally, recertification should be an easy process. For a lifeguard who keeps her knowledge and skills up to date, recertification should be no problem. However, not all lifeguards remain in top mental and physical condition year-round.

For some people, lifeguarding is a seasonal job, with a long break during off-season winter months. Other individuals find their lifeguarding career inter-rupted by school or military obligations. And some lifeguards simply don't stay in shape, possibly even failing recertification trials. For these lifeguards, activities and games can make reentry a more satisfying process. Variety, chal-lenge, stimulation, and enjoyment can make skill review and text study not only pleasant but also rewarding. Through activities and games, lifeguards learn new applications for previously learned emergency response skills.

At certain times, all lifeguards must also retrain in order to learn new skills. Lifeguarding is not a stagnant discipline. As new equipment is developed and medical science expands its approaches to saving lives, lifeguards must update their personal skills to keep pace with state-of-the-art methods and techniques. It is easier for people to learn a new skill if that skill can be applied in a context that they already know. The activities and games in this book are not technique specific. Rather, they can be used with existing procedures as well as with emer-gency response systems and schematics that may be developed in the future.

Using Activities and Games to Develop Leadership

Leadership development begins on the very first day an individual—a future lifeguard—arrives at your pool, regardless of the person's age. Leadership training begins when a young child adopts a role model in the aquatic setting, whether that role model is a lifeguard, an instructor, an older participant, or a skilled peer. Leadership development can begin the first time a child hears an explanation of pool rules. Leadership development is already in progress when a person remembers to shower before entering the water, or to walk rather than run on deck. Leadership training is part of the experience of aquatic participa-tion, including the participation of lifeguards in professional training activities.

The initiation of formal leadership training should depend on several factors, including the person's chronological age, developmental age, and social and psychological maturity. Chronologically, employment as a lifeguard can usually begin at age 16. However, not all 16-year-olds are developmentally, socially, and psychologically mature enough for employment in a position of such responsibility. In fact, some people—even well into adulthood—will never be ready for the responsibilities associated with being a lifeguard.

One of the bases for judgment of maturity is a person's ability to make good decisions. Also consider how a young person is regarded by his peers. Do they look to him as a leader? This could be positive or negative. However, even with a teen who appears to have negative leadership tendencies, investing in leadership development can have positive results over the long process.

In addition, consider how a child responds to leadership by others, particularly leadership that results in the application of behavioral restrictions. Can the youth handle hearing the word *no*? To become a leader, a person must first be agreeable to being led, even in unpleasant circumstances. Respect for authority is an important quality for future leaders.

By implementing lifeguarding activities and games, you can provide numerous leadership opportunities for your lifeguards. Here are some suggestions:

- Let your more senior lifeguards know that during training activities, you expect them to be performance examples for new staff. This makes your senior staff informal leaders, and it gives each of them more responsibility for the success of your facility's lifeguard team.
- Once an activity is running, rotate the person who goes first, sets the pace, is team captain, or provides directions. Through rotation, everyone gets an opportunity to try her leadership wings.
- When analyzing participants' performance in an activity, include discussion of leadership and how the leader contributed or detracted from success.
- Be sure everyone has a chance to lead something. Nothing is more demoralizing to a group of employees than when most members think they are in a subclass in relation to a few favorites. Work to bring out the leadership potential in *all* lifeguards.
- Develop a hierarchy of leadership tasks, ranging from something simple such as putting out equipment to conducting an entire morning of in-service training. Performing leadership tasks that are increasingly more challenging will help keep your lifeguards invested in the program, while also strengthening their personal self-esteem.
- Provide your senior lifeguards with a copy of this book, and assign them the task of selecting and conducting conditioning activities.

Yes, your lifeguards can assist in the training and conditioning of other lifeguards. You should expect an assistant head lifeguard or assistant aquatic program director to already have achieved an appropriate skill level in the area for which he will be assisting. For example, a lifeguard who has achieved the highest level of physical condition would be the most logical choice to lead conditioning activities. Leadership tasks that your lifeguards can assist with include the following:

- Taking attendance and performing lifeguard check-in
- Preparing equipment for a training session
- Fetching equipment during a training session or putting equipment away at the end of the session

- Demonstrating tasks in an activity or game
- Participating with a new lifeguard or weaker staff member in paired skill drills
- Performing peer coaching
- Planning or leading an activity or game
- Supervising small-group activities or games (while you work with a different group)
- Taking notes on individual or group performance in order to help plan future activities

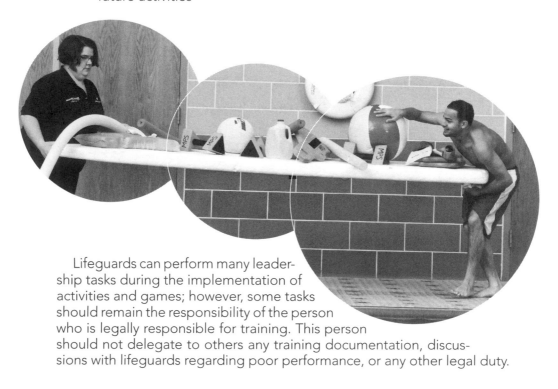

Lifeguards can perform many leadership tasks during the implementation of activities and games; however, some tasks should remain the responsibility of the person who is legally responsible for training. This person should not delegate to others any training documentation, discussions with lifeguards regarding poor performance, or any other legal duty.

Selecting Appropriate Activities

Lap swimming is the most common method of conditioning used in advanced aquatics, and it serves the purposes of conditioning. However, swimming laps can be tedious, particularly for those who need conditioning the most. In addition, some people will take much longer to lap swim than others, having no incentive to be efficient because more of the same old activities will follow. Varying the conditioning activities used will increase interest and break monotony. Everyone can participate for the same amount of time, and then everyone can move on to another activity. In addition, when conditioning activities are based on essential lifeguard skills, the activities enhance skill learning. Keeping fun and challenge in the training process increases enjoyment and furthers participation, while continually reinforcing skilled performance.

Lap swimming is not directly related to other skills that lifeguards must accomplish. Many people enter lifeguarding thinking that being a strong or fast swimmer is all it takes to be a successful lifeguard. But experienced lifeguards know that they must be able to do a variety of other things in addition to being a good swimmer. For example, lifeguards must be able to do the following:

- Keep a heavy victim afloat
- Submerge quickly and stay under water while searching
- Execute specific skills with a high level of accuracy, even with a nose and mouth full of water, a leg cramp, or a feeling of fear in one's soul
- Perform at a high level of physical and mental response and with high accuracy even when fatigued
- Think in action, and respond with finely honed motor skills to unforeseen circumstances
- Demonstrate proper behaviors as a role model for other lifeguards, as well as for all aquatic participants
- Function as a contributing member of a highly trained team

Lifeguard activities and games are skill related. They present a great variety of opportunities for enhancing specific lifeguarding skills. Movement flexibility, comfort on and under the water, endurance, and strength combine with knowledge and attitude to mold a strong, fast swimmer into a proficient lifeguard.

Each person entering lifeguard training comes with her own individual goals, needs, preconceptions, skills, strengths, and weaknesses. Each lifeguard on your team also has personal characteristics that will influence how she performs as a lifeguard. Transformation into an experienced, highly competent lifeguard can be an easy process, or it can be a process with many hardships. Successes and accomplishments create positive environments. Activities and games enhance the potential for success and accomplishment. The specific activities and games you select should depend on your purpose. Activities and games provide opportunities to do the following:

- Overcome discouragement and dissatisfaction with training. Training through fun activities and games can also make it easier to engage individuals who are used to getting praise, high marks, or other positive reinforcement while exerting little effort. Lifeguarding requires a strong effort in emergency response, no matter how good a swimmer the lifeguard is.

- Apply textbook information. For example, a lifeguard must be able to submerge quickly to execute an escape if being grabbed by a victim. But, how quick is quick? A game such as Leapfrog helps lifeguards learn how to perform a quick, unexpected submersion.

- Practice a single skill in a variety of application scenarios. For example, a stride jump or compact jump and swim can be used in a relay, for a rescue scenario, and for the Swim and Reverse activity. These are all ways of reinforcing the same skill, without repetitive skill practice.

- Break the seriousness of training and relieve stress. Constant attention to detail and perfection can be stressful. In school, a grade of 70 percent is usually a C (or average), which is a passing grade. When skills are tested in physical education, passing 7 out of 10 skills may also be acceptable. However, no one wants her life (or her child's life) to depend on a lifeguard who has only mastered 70 or 75 percent of the required skills. In lifeguarding, as in no other physical activity, the standard for passing—the point where success is achieved—is much higher. All skills (100 percent) must be mastered, and written test scores must usually be above 80 percent (although this will vary from program to program). This can mean a great deal of stress for the lifeguard in training, as well as for the aging lifeguard who must maintain certification. Activities and games are fun, and they are great for relieving training stress.

• Develop teamwork. When an activity or game requires group effort and cooperation, lifeguards learn that success depends on each individual giving his best effort for the group purpose. This is an important value for lifeguards to develop and hold.

• Prepare lifeguards for unpredictable future events. No one can predict exactly how an emergency response incident will unfold. Lifeguards must be able to adapt immediately to unforeseen circumstances.

• Prepare lifeguards to accept failure. Sometimes even the very best efforts fail. We are a culture of winners. Activities and games often include failure in the face of a person's best effort. These activities help lifeguards develop the capacity to learn from unsuccessful efforts and experiences, thus helping them to plan for the future.

• Provide leadership opportunities. Leadership opportunities enhance the professional growth of young people who want to move up the ladder in the aquatic profession. From swimmers in advanced stroke classes to junior guards, on through lifeguard training, and upward into lifeguard supervision and aquatic management, leadership opportunity is key to advancement. Activities and games provide these leadership opportunities.

Although activities and games can fulfill each of the previous purposes, you must determine and target specific training goals and objectives on a daily basis. These targets include the following:

• Physical conditioning, including building strength, increasing endurance, developing flexibility, and improving cardiorespiratory capacity

• Safety awareness, including becoming more aware of safety as an aquatic participant and becoming a lifeguard who can elicit and develop safety awareness in others

• Skill development and practice, including water rescue skills, equipment handling, CPR skills, and first aid

• Emergency response enhancement, including surveillance, recognition of emergent situations, response team activation, and response coordination

• Teamwork facilitation, including peer interaction, use of the chain of command, and leadership development

• Stress reduction and relaxation, including the release of tension as well as just plain enjoyment

Once you determine your goals and objectives, you should use the activity finder on page vi to identify activities or games that can be used to meet your specific needs. Categories on the activity selection chart are similar to the chapter titles in this book. Keep in mind that an activity or game can serve more than one purpose. That is why you will find some activities and games listed in more than one category. Use the activity finder to maximize your time in training by meeting as many goals as possible.

Conducting Effective Activities

Many excellent activities have gone unappreciated by participants because of boredom, low morale, lack of understanding of goals, or a general negative atmosphere. The aquatic leader, head lifeguard, or program manager must ensure that each participant gets maximum benefit for the time and effort spent in the activity. Here are some suggestions that can help you get the best results from any activity or game:

- Vary the type of equipment used. Although it may be necessary to repeat an activity, varying the equipment adds additional challenges and keeps repetition from becoming boring.

- Vary the number of pieces of equipment used in an activity or game. Having one piece of equipment moving at a time is the easiest. The more equipment moving at one time, the more difficult the task.

- Alter the degree of competition. Keeping track of winners and losers may or may not be part of the activity. Most strong swimmers enjoy the intrinsic challenge of the game itself. Let the mood of the group determine whether or not a score is kept.

- Stress the cooperative nature of activities. The goal is to enhance the abilities of everyone in the group. Lifeguards work as a team, so they need everyone on the team to be strong and capable. Emphasize how an activity benefits everyone.

- Keep the focus on positives. Emphasize the number of successful repetitions, as opposed to misses. Emphasize the time sustained, as opposed to time missed. Keep participants moving forward and feeling successful. Avoid focusing on negatives and making participants feel like failures.

- If an activity requires repetitions, start with a low number of reps, and gradually increase the reps. An alternative to increased repetitions is to reduce the time allotted for completion of a task.

- Tell participants the purpose of the activity. Part of being a successful lifeguard is being able to maintain fitness after certification. Understanding the purpose of an activity helps lifeguards build a repertoire of ways to maintain their own personal fitness level.

- Maintain an atmosphere of play. These activities should be fun. Lifeguards must be serious about many things. Maintaining personal fitness, sharpening response time, and honing skills are critical. How this is accomplished does not have to be totally serious. Keep the fun in difficult and challenging tasks, and lifeguards are more likely to engage in those tasks frequently.

- Remember that even an excellent activity can go wrong, no matter how well implemented the activity or how enthusiastic the participants. If a negative situation occurs, you should use debriefing. Through your modeling of the debriefing process, your lifeguards will learn a valuable tool for resolving negative situations. At the same time, you will be able to defuse a negative situation and restore a positive training environment.

- Be sure your activities and games are as well planned as every other aspect of your lifeguarding program. Proper planning tells your lifeguards how much value you place on the activity. This should include taking the time to plan ahead, having equipment organized ahead of time, providing a sound explanation of the activity and why participation is important, monitoring the execution of the activity, and, finally, analyzing with your lifeguards how performance in the activity or game went. If you complete these planning tasks, your lifeguards will benefit more from their participation, and they will also be much more likely to replicate the activity for their own conditioning or practice.

Challenging activities can become stressful. Fatigue, lack of fitness, and even staying out late the night before an activity can lead to performance that is less than optimal. Furthermore, helping individuals develop optimal performance often involves taking them to the absolute limit of their current performance level, and then challenging them to go further. Challenge can lead to stress. Stress can lead to negativity. Negativity can endanger performance in the tasks that a lifeguard needs to master. This can drive a potentially good lifeguard out of the field. Here are some of the signs that negativity is developing among participants:

- Participants wanting to quit well before reaching their performance limits
- Extreme harassment of each other
- Crying
- Injuries

- Illness or vomiting
- Sulking or silent behavior
- Totally inappropriate responses during an activity
- Hazing
- Bullying of another participant
- Using offensive language
- Responding disrespectfully to the activity leader
- Damage to equipment

Although stress of the moment can bring out negative characteristics in a person, such characteristics have no place in the behavior of lifeguards. Lifeguards must face stress continually. Each lifeguard must be able to control his own behaviors before he can be responsible for the behavior and lives of others. A lifeguard must be able to accept and participate in situations that he might not like, including accepting criticism during training or accepting unwelcome discipline from a leader. There are appropriate as well as inappropriate ways to respond to negative situations. Negative situations in training must be recognized and resolved in a timely manner for the welfare of all. To resolve a negative situation during an activity or game, you may use several stages of remediation:

Stage 1   Discontinue the current activity, and discuss with the group or individual why the activity was halted. Encourage participants to bring up negative aspects, as well as how the situation can be improved. Then begin the activity again. If better results occur, continue the activity. If negative results still occur, discontinue the activity or change to some other activity.

Stage 2   Discontinue the activity, and change to something else. At a later time, when all participants have had a chance to decompress, discuss the activity and the negative results. Then try the activity again on another day.

Stage 3   Discontinue the activity, and change to something else. At a later time, meet with and counsel the specific individuals who contributed to the negative results of the group (this meeting should take place away from the rest of the group). Then try the activity again on another day.

Stage 4   Stop the activity temporarily, and remove the individuals who seem to be creating negative results. Later, meet with these individuals privately. Also, discuss the situation with the rest of the group. Work to resolve differences that lead to negative situations. Note: Discontinuing an activity in any given circumstance should not be viewed as giving in to lifeguards who do not like the activity. Continuing an activity or game in a negative atmosphere is of little benefit, and doing so could lead to an accident or injury. Discontinuing should be viewed merely as a postponement until a later time when the atmosphere will be more conducive to productive engagement.

Stage 5   Repeated negative situations indicate serious adjustment problems. After seeing what the ongoing job is all about, some lifeguards realize that lifeguarding isn't really what they want to do, even though they have obtained certification. These individuals should be counseled to move into some other aquatic pursuit. For lifeguards, teamwork is vital. If a lifeguard is unable to work as part of a team, including during training activities and games, that lifeguard may need to seek employment elsewhere. A lifeguard corps is not a place for an individual to let personal feelings get in the way of team efforts.

Contacting the parents of a lifeguard is sometimes an option. Because lifeguards can be hired at age 16 in some areas, some of your lifeguard employees may be minors under the law. In some cases, a lifeguard might still be in high school. Not all lifeguards are adults, even though they are fulfilling adult job roles.

Be aware that the parents have often provided funds to cover the costs of lifeguard training for their son or daughter—with the goal that this training will lead to a job that will look very good on a resume. Parents often assume that their child getting hired is the end result, giving little thought to ongoing job performance. However, if their child receives a poor job evaluation, gets fired, or gets injured on the job, the parents will certainly take an interest.

You should always make every attempt to solve problems without contacting a parent. After all, the parent will not be on the guard stand when the youth must respond to an emergency. However, minor-age lifeguards are just that—legal minors under the jurisdiction of their parents. The process of becoming an adult is ongoing. Sometimes the parent of a lifeguard can provide you with valuable insight and support. When contacting a parent, you should do the following:

- Identify yourself, your program, and how you and your program relate to the parent's child. Sometimes children enter employment without their parents' knowledge or consent.

- Begin with a statement of praise or a positive statement about the child's participation. This gets the conversation off to a good start so that the parent is in an agreeable position.

- Provide a summary statement of the problem as you see it, including how that problem is affecting the job performance of the youth. Follow by asking the parent if he is aware of the problem. Be brief, but factual; avoid inflammatory language and exaggeration.

- Be prepared to provide specific examples of the problem, including the date, circumstances, and result.

- Ask the parent for suggestions on how to alleviate the problem. You may learn a lot about the youth, as well as get good advice. After all, the parent has been dealing with this youth for much longer than you have.

- If the parent seems unconvinced, consider inviting the parent to visit the program and observe (unknown to the youth, if possible).

- Provide a summary of the possible consequences, such as patron injury or peer staff negativity hindering teamwork if the situation does not resolve. Be sure to include response for the consequences. This might include not only a negative job evaluation, but also eventual job termination.

- Assure the parent that you are available for future consultation. The parent may want time to speak with the youth and then report back to you.

Contact with a parent can also help identify employment goals. Ideally, goals of the employee, goals of the parents, and goals of your program will match, focusing on successful job performance of a qualified lifeguard. However, if these goals do *not* match, problems may result. Resolving goal mismatches may also help resolve any training difficulties. Successful participation in the ongoing job training that you provide—including your activities and games—is an integral part of overall job performance. Lifeguards and parents need to understand this.

Remember, a parent can be your best advocate—or your worst enemy. Obviously, having the parent as your advocate is much preferable. How you handle the contact with the parent can make the difference.

Is this a lot of work? Most certainly. Would you be inclined to do this for a lifeguard of legal age? Of course not. However, the nature of the job of lifeguard, combined with the age at which a person can be hired for the job, creates a state of limbo that requires employers to operate with caution.

Safety and Risk Management

Although the major focus in lifeguarding is usually on making rescues, safety and good risk management are really the keys to effective aquatic operations. How you maintain safety and manage risk within your employee training program tells your lifeguards the value you place on safe operations. It also serves as a model for your lifeguards regarding how much importance they should place on accident prevention and creating a safe environment for aquatic participants. You must be a good example!

Safety is critical in all lifeguard training activities. Participants should be safe at all times. Whoever is leading the activity should be a role model when it comes to safety. Safety should never be compromised for reasons of fun. No conditioning or learning goals should be attained at the expense of participant safety. The following suggestions can help reduce the risk of injury:

- Make sure that a lifeguard is on duty during all lifeguard training and in-service activities. Even competent swimmers can have life-threatening accidents. Training drills are often designed to stretch individual capabilities. You must be safe. Have a lifeguard. You can integrate having a lifeguard on duty with the training activities. Assign numbers to the participants. Call out the numbers in sequence every few minutes; the person whose number is called rotates into the lifeguard position and becomes the guard on duty. The other participants watch and then comment on the effectiveness of the rotation.

- Before initiating training, warn participants of the inherent dangers present in the training activity. Also warn them of the consequences for unsafe actions. In your training plans, document that you have provided this warning.

- Use graduated depth progressions for all drills that involve practicing water rescue skills. Introduce new skills on land first, then move to shallow water, and finally to deep water.

- Use an unresponsive to responsive victim protocol for all drills that involve practicing water rescue skills. Begin with an unresponsive victim. Increase the mobility and responsiveness of the victim only when participants have mastered control of an unresponsive victim.

- Have a safety signal for STOP. Three taps or pinches are traditionally the personal signal for "Let go!" Be sure everyone knows a deck signal, such as a long blast of the whistle, for calling a halt to an activity. Sometimes the group leader sees a dangerous situation that is unknown to participants in the water. That person must also be able to bring an immediate stop to any activity.

- Do not allow participants to wear any jewelry. This includes body piercing jewelry (internal or external). Taping jewelry is *not* appropriate, because tape can come off.

- When multiple pieces of equipment are in use, be sure all swimmers know when equipment is added. Also make sure that swimmers know what they should visually focus on.

- When an activity involves throwing, be sure the object thrown cannot hurt the swimmer if the catch is missed.

- Teach participants that when they are throwing an object to another person, they must be sure that the person is looking before making the throw. Calling the person's name before a throw is a good way to focus attention.

- Do not allow participants to wear competitive swim goggles for submersion in water deeper than 5 feet (152 cm). Pressure differentials can cause eye damage.
- Do not allow participants to wear competitive swim goggles for any victim contact work.
- Do not allow participants to wear nose clips for any rescue work.
- Do not allow participants to wear eyeglasses or contact lenses for any victim contact work. Although glasses or sunglasses may be worn by guards on duty, wearing glasses for victim contact practice is dangerous to the wearer as well as the victim.
- Do not allow participants to perform repeated deep breathing (designed to increase oxygen content of the blood) before underwater swimming.
- Limit underwater activities and do not conduct activities that include breath-holding contests.
- Encourage participants to discuss desired outcomes. Winning at all costs is not appropriate in lifeguard training activities.
- Make sure that equipment is always used appropriately. Discourage participants from using equipment for purposes that it was not intended to be used.

Ultimately, you must conduct your training activities with the same high level of safety and risk management that you want your lifeguards to use as they go about their job. You are the best example they can have. Be the safety-conscious leader you want your lifeguards to be.

Documenting Training Activities

Lifeguarding activities and games represent more than time fillers or training add-ons. Although many of the activities in this book take only a few minutes and are fun to participate in, each activity plays a valuable part in the ongoing training necessary to keep a lifeguard staff at peak capability. Therefore, the activities and games should be documented as part of the training record for each individual, as well as the records for the facility or program. The documentation for each individual should include the following:

- Date of training
- Training leader
- Name of the activity
- Purpose of the activity
- Performance rating for the individual
- Deficiencies noted
- Projected date of recheck on deficiencies
- Additional notes regarding remediation taken for deficiencies that are not promptly resolved

An individual record should also include a place for the signature of the trainer and the individual participant. You should photocopy each report. Give one copy to the participant for his records, and file one copy in a personnel file. This record of individual training is important for documenting the actions you take to maintain a highly trained staff. It is also critical to the termination process if you have to release a lifeguard from employment. See page 17 for a sample individual training record.

Be sure to note each activity and the result in your training records, even if the activity is short and its purpose is just for fun. Every activity and game in this book has a training purpose that can contribute to building a highly effective lifeguard team.

Documentation of group training requires slightly different information. See the group training record on page 18. Group documentation should include the following:

- Date and time of training
- Whether this is regularly scheduled training or something else, such as incident follow-up training
- Location of training
- Training leader
- Training participants
- Training activities (activity and purpose)
- Complete lesson plan for training, including a list of all activities and games, along with the purpose for each
- Notes regarding any unusual incidents or personnel conflicts that occurred during training
- Results of training (noting strengths and weaknesses of the group as well as individuals)
- Projections for future training

Sample Individual Training Record

Name: Liam O'Connor

RATING SCALE:
5 = superior, 4 = above average, 3 = acceptable, 2 = not acceptable, 1 = poor

Date	Activity	Purpose	Rating	Deficiencies	Recheck	Leader
6/12	Lap Chase Tag	Swim speed	5	None	None	R. Kaye
6/12	Brick-Ups	Treading water, endurance, and strength	3	Form of kick incorrect, resulting in more effort required	7/12 (check for kick form and increased endurance)	R. Kaye
7/12	Brick-Ups	Treading recheck	4	Form now correct, endurance needed	8/12 (check for endurance)	R. Kaye
7/12	Accident Reports	Accurate records & reports	2	Incorrect data; illegible handwriting	7/20 (check for data and legible handwriting)	R. Kaye
7/20	Accident Reports	Accurate records & reports	4	Data correct; handwriting better	None	R. Kaye
8/12	Brick-Ups	Treading endurance	5	None	None	R. Kaye

Additional Remediation Plan Notes
Include here any additional performance-related notes.

Lifeguard signature _____ Date _____

_____ Date _____

_____ Date _____

_____ Date _____

_____ Date _____

From Susan J. Grosse, 2009, *Lifeguard Training Activities and Games* (Champaign, IL: Human Kinetics).

Group Training Record

Date: _____ Time: _____ Location: _____

Regular training: _____ Yes _____ No

If no, reason for training: _____

Training leader: _____

Participants (enter names or attach list):

_____

_____

Training Activities (Lesson Plan Must Be Attached)

Activity	Purpose
1.	
2.	
3.	
4.	

Training Results

Strengths	Weaknesses

Unusual incidents: _____

Training follow-up: _____

Record completed by: _____ Date: _____

From Susan J. Grosse, 2009, *Lifeguard Training Activities and Games* (Champaign, IL: Human Kinetics).

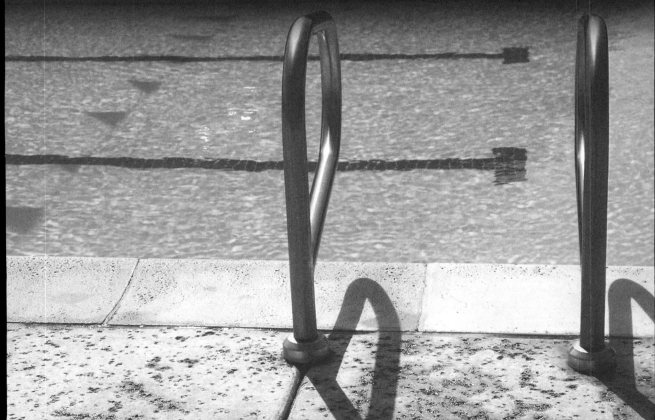

2

Conditioning
Activities

The activities and games in this chapter emphasize physical conditioning—the development of endurance, strength, flexibility, and cardiorespiratory fitness. Without physical conditioning, a lifeguard's rescue skills would be meaningless. A lifeguard must be in peak physical condition at all times. Lap swims are traditional. And everyone has favorite drills that focus on treading water. Over time, these activities become boring, and bored swimmers do not work at optimal levels. Although laps and treading do help maintain fitness, this is all they do. An activity or game can contribute to conditioning while also helping lifeguards to bridge from conditioning to skill applications. Activities and games reinforce skills and enable lifeguards to maintain fitness while avoiding boredom.

A lifeguard's physical conditioning contributes directly to the success of any rescue. Here's how physical conditioning contributes to the lifeguard's performance:

• Endurance is the capability to sustain strenuous activity. Endurance enables the lifeguard to swim distances, repeat actions, and sustain energy output over a prolonged period of time. This is particularly important for lifeguards at open-water facilities, those who must make repeated water rescues, and lifeguards working longer hours.

• Strength is the capability to move, lift, and carry heavy objects. Strength enables the lifeguard to tow a victim to safety and lift that victim from the water, whether using a backboard or not. Strength is especially important when a lifeguard is working with a victim who is larger than the lifeguard, a victim who is nonbuoyant, or a victim who is unresponsive.

• Flexibility is the capability to move major joints through as full a range of motion as possible. Flexibility enables a lifeguard to adjust his body position as needed to effectively maintain a safe position in the water. It also enables a lifeguard to complete a rescue with maximum efficiency. This is particularly important for a lifeguard in a situation requiring the use of an escape. Flexibility is also important when working on land during resuscitation. In this situation, good flexibility allows the lifeguard to effectively move from performing CPR to using an AED to providing first aid.

• Cardiorespiratory fitness is the capability of the circulatory and respiratory systems to work together to deliver oxygen and remove waste products, particularly during times of peak motor output. Having a high level of cardiorespiratory fitness enables a lifeguard to respond with the greatest physical efficiency. This type of fitness is particularly important when a guard must make the transition from sitting in a guard chair for a prolonged period to the instant, full-energy response required during an emergency.

Because they are unique and challenging, activities and games inspire participants to perform the necessary conditioning work. Participants focus on the challenge of the activity rather than on the strenuous aspects of participation. When participants are challenged, they do not become bored or lax in performance.

Conditioning games and activities can be used at the start of a water session or as a quick warm-up after practicing a relatively stationary skill, such as backboarding. You can also intersperse these activities throughout the training session in order to provide a mental break or a transition of focus. A conditioning activity may be used at the conclusion of a water workout to add something fun to an otherwise serious rescue practice.

ARM TREAD

EQUIPMENT   None

DESCRIPTION   Participants tread water using just their arms. Each participant's body must remain vertical; the legs should be straight and together, extended from the hips. The participant's head must be kept above water. The arm action used is sculling just under the surface of the water (as if spreading frosting on a cake).

VARIATIONS

- Participants perform sculling without bending the elbows.
- Participants vary their body position by tucking the knees to the chest, flexing the legs at the hip while keeping the knees straight (L-sit), or using the straddle sit.
- While arm treading, participants turn in a circle or move from place to place.
- While arm treading, participants perform a lower body exercise (such as alternating knee tucks to the chest with full leg extensions) as quickly as possible.

AVOID IT

EQUIPMENT   One tethered buoy

DESCRIPTION   Participants join hands to form a circle while treading in deep water. The buoy ball is anchored in the center of the circle. On a predetermined signal, each participant attempts to pull someone else into contact with the tethered buoy ball—at the same time, each person tries to avoid being pulled into contact with the buoy.

Once someone touches the ball, that person must swim a penalty or do deck push-ups while the other participants form the circle again and repeat the activity. Once the penalty is completed, the person may rejoin the circle.

VARIATIONS

- Vary the object anchored in the center. The smaller the object, the more difficult it will be to pull a participant into contact with it.
- Change the penalty, emphasizing something that will help participants improve their weaknesses.
- Have participants grasp wrists instead of hands.
- Free hands and have participants create waves to move the ball away from themselves until it touches another person.

BOARD OR BAR PUSH

EQUIPMENT   Rescue board, kickboard, or Aquafit Bar

DESCRIPTION   Two swimmers position themselves at opposite ends of a rescue board or kickboard. The swimmers should have their hands on the end corners of the board, with their arms extended. On a signal, each swimmer begins kicking and tries to force the opposite swimmer to back up a measured distance. Make sure that swimmers are not backed into pool walls. Remind swimmers to keep their arms straight in order to avoid getting the board in their teeth.

VARIATIONS

- Use an Aquafit Bar in place of a kickboard. An Aquafit Bar is a rod covered with foam (similar to the foam of an aquatic noodle), with the rod ends extending out on either end of the foam—it is somewhat like an aqua noodle with a bar inside.

...continued

- Have swimmers compete in a team board push. Place three or four swimmers on opposite long sides of the rescue board.
- Specify the type of kick to be used (flutter kick, breaststroke kick, or even a vertical scissors kick).
- Add a brick to the top of the board, and have swimmers perform the Board Push while trying not to let the brick slide off. Use bricks that weigh 5, 10, or 20 pounds (2.3, 4.5, or 9.1 kg). Vary the brick weight for added challenge.
- Add a plastic glass full of water to the top of the board, and have swimmers perform the Board Push while trying not to spill any water. If kickboards are used, have several pairs of participants working at the same time. Add a glass of water to each board. Then, on a given signal, each pair does the Board Push to determine who can push their opposite person to the designated place first—and also with the least amount of water spill.

BOUNCE-UPS

EQUIPMENT One scuba weight belt for each participant; a variety of slide-on weights ranging from 1 to 3 pounds (0.5 to 1.4 kg)

DESCRIPTION Each participant puts on a scuba weight belt. Several slide-on weights should be added to each belt. The number of weights to add will be determined by the buoyancy of the participant. The more buoyant the individual, the more weight should be added. An extremely buoyant person may need 8 to 10 pounds (3.6 to 4.5 kg). Participants should distribute the weight evenly around the belt, and the belt should be worn just on top of the pelvic bones.

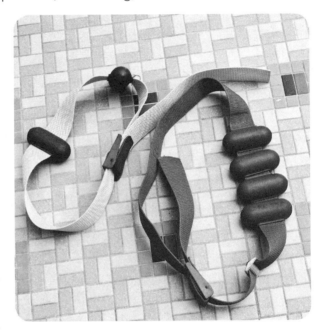

Once the belt is in place, participants execute a feet-first surface dive, touch the bottom with their feet, and then swim back to the surface as quickly as possible. Caution: Remind swimmers that they should return to the surface with one hand up when practicing feetfirst surface dives; this will help them avoid a collision with any object or person on the surface. When reaching the bottom, swimmers may touch down deep, bending the knees and getting close to the bottom surface. Then they will be able to use the bottom to push off in order to assist in their ascent. The weight belt will assist in the feetfirst surface dive, helping buoyant individuals get a feel for performance of an efficient feetfirst dive. The belt will impede the swimmer's return to the surface because of the added weight. Participants must work harder to reach the surface, thus improving their capability to bring up a heavy victim during a rescue of a submerged victim.

VARIATIONS

- Add retrieval of a 10-pound brick from the bottom to the sequence.
- Have participants perform the activity while fully clothed (with or without a weight belt). This provides a more even distribution of additional weight.
- Have participants wear the weight belt or clothing during practice of submerged victim rescues.

BRICK PASS

EQUIPMENT   One 5-, 10-, or 20-pound brick

DESCRIPTION   Swimmers tread water in a circle formation. Treading swimmers pass a brick around the circle. If the brick is dropped, the person who dropped it must retrieve it. The brick cannot be tossed. It must be handed. On a predetermined signal, participants must change the direction of the pass.

VARIATIONS
- Have swimmers pass more than one brick at a time. Start each brick going in a different direction.
- Do not allow the brick to get wet while it is being passed.
- Require each swimmer to do a specified number of Brick-Ups (see the next activity) when receiving the brick.
- Have swimmers pair up and pass the brick between just two people. They should count the number of passes occurring during a specific time period.
- Require swimmers to vary their hand positions, sometimes using only one hand (keeping the other arm across the chest) and sometimes using two hands.
- For added challenge, vary the weight of the brick used (5, 10, or 20 pounds).
- Have participants perform the activity blindfolded.

BRICK-UPS

EQUIPMENT   One 5-, 10-, or 20-pound brick for each swimmer

DESCRIPTION   Each swimmer treads water while holding a brick with both hands at the surface of the water. While treading, the swimmer lifts the brick overhead until the arms are straight, and then lowers the brick back to the surface. A swimmer's face should not submerge. Swimmers should attempt to perform 10 repetitions without a face dunk.

VARIATIONS

- Swimmers hold their brick in the elevated position for a specified number of seconds on each lift.
- Swimmers count the lifts out loud. Swimmers could also sing a verse of a song while performing Brick-Ups.
- Rather than counting lifts, swimmers perform lifts for a specific time period.
- Swimmers do Brick-Ups with only one arm; the other arm is used to scull (if assistance is needed) or is placed across the chest (if assistance is not needed). Swimmers can also do Brick-Ups with alternating arms.
- Swimmers perform Brick-Ups while doing a specified kick.
- The weight of the brick used can be varied for added challenge (5, 10, or 20 pounds).
- Brick-Ups can also be included in other activities, such as the Brick Pass.

BRICK-UPS ROTATIONS AND RELAYS (R & Rs)

EQUIPMENT   One 5-, 10-, or 20-pound brick

DESCRIPTION   Swimmers form a line in deep water, parallel to one wall of the pool. All swimmers tread water (with or without using their hands). A swimmer at one end of the line has the brick. This swimmer begins by doing five Brick-Ups (see the previous activity) and then passing the brick to the next person in line. After passing the brick, the swimmer then moves to the opposite end of the line by swimming Travel Treads (see page 58) with hands on shoulders. The next person performs the same sequence, and the pattern repeats until the first person is back in place at her original end of the line. To keep the line in the same place, swimmers must move sideward with each pass. Each swimmer must do Brick-Ups before passing the brick.

VARIATIONS

- Divide swimmers into two teams, and have them compete to see which team can be first to complete the pattern.
- Require swimmers to turn in place while performing the Brick-Up.
- Add a second task to the Brick-Up—for example, swimmers perform five Brick-Ups, pass the brick under their knees, and then pass it on.
- Conduct the activity as a shuttle relay by positioning swimmers in two lines, end to end, with space between ends. Start a brick at the front of each line. After the initial Brick-Ups, the first swimmer passes the brick to the next person in her line, but instead of going to the end of her own line, the swimmer crosses to the end of the opposite line (swimming Travel Treads).
- For added challenge, vary the weight of the brick used (5, 10, or 20 pounds).

CAGE BALL PASS

EQUIPMENT   Cage ball (Note: If a cage ball is not available, a buoy ball, balance ball, or earth ball may be easily substituted.)

DESCRIPTION   Swimmers tread water in a circle. A cage ball is passed overhead around the group. The ball cannot touch the surface of the water. Swimmers must pass the ball using two hands. The ball should not be thrown or batted.

VARIATIONS
- Add music to the activity. When the music stops, the person with the ball must hold it in the air for a specific number of seconds (or until the music starts again).
- Increase the distances between swimmers, forcing each swimmer to perform a Travel Tread (see page 58) while holding the ball overhead in order to pass it on.
- Have participants pair up and pass the ball back and forth between two people. See how many passes each pair can make in a specified time.

CLOTHES CAPER

EQUIPMENT   Long trousers, a long-sleeved shirt, and tennis shoes for each participant (Note: Items should be clean and safe for pool use.)

DESCRIPTION   Wearing clothes over their swimsuits, participants jump into deep water, disrobe, and drop their clothes to the bottom of the pool. Then each person retrieves his clothes and puts them back on again. A survival float can be used during disrobing and putting clothing back on. Teach participants that they should remove the heaviest item first. Participants wearing pullover shirts should be taught to gather the shirt under their armpits and remove their arms before pulling the shirt over their head.

VARIATIONS

- Participants perform the required tasks within a specified time limit, or they race against each other.
- Participants must swim a specified number of pool lengths before disrobing.
- This activity can also be staged as a relay. Swimmers are divided into teams. Each team has one long-sleeved shirt and one pair of long trousers (size should be sufficient so that every person can get into the selected articles). Shoes are not used for this variation because they are more difficult to size for a group. Teams are lined up, one swimmer behind the other; the two lines are parallel to each other and perpendicular to the pool wall. The first person in line holds the clothes. On a start signal, the first person puts on the clothes and swims out to a designated point (or the opposite side of the pool). This person then returns to his line and removes the clothes, giving them to the next person (or dropping them to the bottom). The first person then moves to the end of the line as the second person takes (or retrieves) the clothes and repeats the action. The winning side is the first to rotate back to its original line. This relay can also be done as a shuttle relay with participants moving to opposite lines on the exchange. Specify the stroke to be used for the swimming portion.
- This activity may also be combined with the Clothing Flotation activity (see page 34).

CLOTHESLINE RELAY

EQUIPMENT   Four clotheslines; four to six clothespins per team; a set of clothes for each team of participants (the set should include long pants, a long-sleeved shirt, socks, and shoes) (Note: Items should be clean and safe for pool use.)

DESCRIPTION   Each clothesline is strung across the width of a six- or eight-lane pool; the clotheslines are placed equidistant from the end walls and each other. Participants are grouped into teams, and each team is given a lane and a set of clothes. To prepare for the relay, the first swimmer swims out to the first clothesline and clips her team's pants to that line. This swimmer then proceeds to the second line and clips on her team's shirt. The swimmer clips the shoes onto the third line and clips the socks onto the last line. When the items have been clipped to all four clotheslines, the swimmer returns to her team. When all teams have prepared their clotheslines, the relay can begin.

On a predetermined signal, the first swimmer swims to the first line, unclips the clothing item found there (in this case, the pants), and puts on the pants while treading water.

After putting on the pants, the swimmer proceeds to the second, third, and fourth lines, putting on clothes at each line (if the shoes are reached before the socks, the swimmer must remove and redo the shoes when the socks are reached). When the swimmer is completely dressed, she completes the swim to the opposite end of the pool, touches the wall, and turns around without standing up. The swimmer then swims back to the starting point, stopping at each successive clothesline, taking off the appropriate item of clothing, and reattaching the item to its original place on the line. When the swimmer—now attired once again in only a swimsuit—reaches the starting spot where her team is

...continued

waiting, she tags the next swimmer and goes to the end of the line. The tagged swimmer now repeats the swim of the first swimmer, putting on clothing at each line, tagging the wall at the far end, returning by disrobing and rehanging the clothes, and tagging the next waiting swimmer. The relay is completed when all swimmers have completed one two-length swim.

VARIATIONS

- Vary the size and fabric weight of the clothing. Clothing that is one size larger than the largest swimmer is easier to put on. However, it will weigh more when wet. Smaller clothing will weigh less but will be more difficult to put on. Fleece is heavier than lightweight cotton.
- Have the swimmers perform blindfolded. The waiting teammates call out directions.
- For added endurance work, require the waiting teammates to tread water while waiting.

Contributed by Ann Wieser, Greensboro, NC

CLOTHES SWIM

EQUIPMENT   Long trousers, a long-sleeved shirt, and tennis shoes for each participant (Note: Items should be clean and safe for pool use.)

DESCRIPTION   Swimmers wear long trousers, a long-sleeved shirt, and tennis shoes in addition to their swimsuits. The swimmers do a lap swim while wearing clothes.

Before the swim, ask participants the following questions:

- What effect will wearing clothes have on swimming?
- When might clothes be left on for swimming?
- When might clothes be removed to facilitate swimming?
- Which articles of clothing are heaviest? Is it always the same type of article?
- What strokes are easiest to swim while wearing clothes?

After the swim, discuss the answers to these questions again.

VARIATIONS

- Have participants wear clothing only on the part of the body that needs conditioning; for example, a participant may wear a sweatshirt to build arm strength or wear sweatpants on the legs to strengthen kick.
- To help swimmers improve endurance, lengthen the distance of the swim.
- Have participants swim against time or swim to cover a specific distance in a specific time.

CLOTHING FLOTATION

EQUIPMENT   A long-sleeved shirt and long trousers for each participant (Note: Items should be clean and safe for pool use.)

DESCRIPTION   Participants enter deep water wearing long-sleeved shirts and long trousers over their swimsuits. They inflate shirts while wearing them using one of two methods: (1) raising the bottom edge of the shirt and splashing air under the front of the shirt or (2) gathering the shirt at the neck and bottom, ducking under water, and blowing air into the shirt through gathers in the neck area. After removing their trousers, participants tie a knot in the bottom of each trouser leg, zip any zipper, gather the waist of the trousers, and blow air into the hole in the gathered waist. Hint: Inflating trousers is just like blowing up a paper bag for popping. Remind participants to tighten their grip around any gathers between breaths. Successfully inflated pants look like two large sausages. In the rest position, the participant's chin is in the crotch of the trousers; the inflated legs are out to the side. The trousers must only support the head.

VARIATIONS

- Add a distance swim after participants enter the water and before they inflate the clothing.
- After inflation, have participants reverse the process and put the trousers back on.
- Combine this activity with the Clothes Caper activities (see page 30).

CLOTHING SCRAMBLE

EQUIPMENT   Long trousers, a long-sleeved shirt, and a pair of tennis shoes for each participant (Note: Items should be clean and safe for pool use.)

DESCRIPTION   At the start of the activity, all participants are told to take a good look at their gear. Then, all clothing items are collected. Participants line up along the side or end of the pool and close their eyes. Then, all of the clothing is dumped into the deep end, out in the middle, making a large pile of items on the pool bottom.

On a predetermined signal, participants open their eyes, sit down, and slide into the water. They swim toward the deep end. Each swimmer's task is to find her own clothing, put on that clothing, and swim back to the start, attempting to be the first person to complete the task. To retrieve clothing from the bottom, participants should use a feetfirst surface dive. When returning to the surface, each person should surface with one arm raised overhead in order to avoid surfacing underneath someone who is treading water or putting on clothing.

VARIATIONS
- Group participants into pairs and tell them to take a good look at their partner's clothing. Ask each participant to retrieve her partner's clothing and then return that clothing to the partner. Each person should then put her own clothing back on.
- Add a clothing inflation task to the sequence, requiring participants to inflate their trousers before putting them on.

CRAFT BY HAND

EQUIPMENT   Canoe, small pram, kayak, or rescue board

DESCRIPTION   Participants must use their hands and arms to propel the equipment. Although rescue boards are hand equipment, the other types of craft are not. When paddles or oars are removed, users must rely on their hands and arms for propulsion. This helps participants develop a feel for what type of propulsive action is required for various types of craft maneuvers. Ask paddlers to move forward and backward in a straight line, make turns, spin circles, perform docking, and sideslip.

VARIATIONS

- Have participants perform as a group or team. This adds the necessity for teamwork. Having four to six people hand-paddle a canoe increases the number of participants and emphasizes working together.
- To make the activity more challenging, require the team of paddlers in each craft to perform blindfolded while a spotter on deck calls out directions.
- Add a time factor. How quickly can the participants navigate the craft through a specific sequence of maneuvers?
- Make the activity an obstacle course.
- Require participants to perform with the craft partially full of water or fully capsized.

FOLLOW THE LEADER

EQUIPMENT   None

DESCRIPTION   Swimmers tread water (they may use their arms). A leader is chosen from the group. That leader performs an activity, and all swimmers follow the leader, repeating the leader's action. The leader may choose any activity desired, as long as he stays in deep water and away from the side of the pool. Allow 15 to 30 repetitions, and then call out a new leader. Activities must vary. New leaders may not repeat an activity that has already been done.

Failure to follow the leader results in a penalty, not exclusion. Change leaders frequently so that everyone gets a chance to lead. Activities may be as creative as the leader can be.

VARIATIONS   Be more specific regarding the types of activities that leaders may select—for example, activities using arms only or legs only, underwater activities, activities using one body part, activities done while singing, or partner activities.

GROUP 500-YARD SWIM

EQUIPMENT   None

DESCRIPTION   Participants are arranged in groups of two or three. Each group is assigned a lane. Their task is to complete a 500-yard (457 m) swim. However, only one member of the team may swim at a time. While one member is swimming, the other two members must tread water at the end of the lane. The first person starts the swim by swimming down to the other end of the pool and back. When this person returns to the starting spot, the second member of the group swims the same distance. When the second person returns, the third person swims down and back, and the whole sequence starts again with the first swimmer. Whenever group members are not lap swimming, they must tread water. The task is completed when 500 yards have been swum.

VARIATIONS

- Increase the number of laps each member must swim before a tradeoff.
- Specify the stroke to be used for each lap segment.
- Time the 500-yard swim, and challenge each group to improve its time.

Contributed by Carrie Paterson, Milwaukee, WI

HAND JIVE

EQUIPMENT   None

DESCRIPTION   Pairs of swimmers tread water, facing each other. Each pair begins with the child's hand game patty-cake. Then each pair makes up their own original patterns of hand claps and slaps, which other pairs of partners must then learn.

When partners are making up patterns, they should start with a specific number of actions. For example, a six-action sequence might be as follows:

1. Clap together.
2. Slap both hands of partner.
3. Slap partner right.
4. Slap partner left.
5. Clap together.
6. Slap both hands of partner.

Heads should remain above the surface at all times. Once the sequence is mastered by the other pairs, the original pair should add a set number of actions. Adding two actions to the previous sequence could result in the following:

1. Clap together.
2. Slap both hands of partner.
3. Slap partner right.
4. Slap partner left.
5. Clap together.
6. Slap both hands of partner.
7. Clap together.
8. Clap together.

...continued

HAND JIVE *...continued*

Swimmers should continue adding actions until the sequence becomes so long that one set of partners cannot replicate the challenge of another.

VARIATIONS

- Have participants perform the clap–slap patterns with uneven beats in order to make it more challenging for other pairs to replicate the pattern.
- Add a song or rhythmic chant to the routine.
- Require participants to vary their arm position from water level to over-head. The farther the arms are above water, the stronger the leg kick will have to be for participants to keep their heads above the surface.

HYDRO UNO

EQUIPMENT   Deck of waterproof Uno cards, card holder, and kickboard

DESCRIPTION Place the cards in the card holder (the type used for regular playing cards). Place the card holder on a kickboard, and float the kickboard and card holder in deep water. This is your playing table. Participants

tread water around the kickboard (table); they should be close enough to reach the cards, but far enough apart that they do not kick each other. Then, participants proceed to play a game of Uno.

The first person out of the game can rest or move to a different activity while the others complete the game. Note that groups of four or five swimmers work best. If additional decks are available, more than one game can be going at one time.

VARIATION   Uno cards come in a waterproof format. You may also laminate cards for other popular card games. Participants can then play those games while treading.

JAMMER CATCH

EQUIPMENT Spin Jammer Frisbee (A Spin Jammer is a specially designed Frisbee that can be spun while held atop one finger. Refer to the list of product suppliers in the appendix.)

DESCRIPTION Swimmers are treading in deep water (they are randomly spaced). One swimmer starts the Spin Jammer spinning on one finger. When the disc is spinning, the swimmer finger-tosses the Spin Jammer to another swimmer. The receiving swimmer catches the disc on one finger, keeps it spinning, and passes it to another swimmer.

VARIATIONS

- Have each swimmer toss and catch to herself. Each swimmer must keep the Jammer spinning on one finger throughout.
- Count the number of passes (to self or to another swimmer) the participants make without a drop. For a group drill, count the number of passes among the group without a miss. All swimmers must receive and pass once before any can receive a second time.
- Specify the number of passes that the participants must complete in a set amount of time.
- Have swimmers pair up and perform partner passes while traveling a width or length of the pool.

KEEP IT UP!

EQUIPMENT   Beach ball

DESCRIPTION   While treading water, each participant must continually set the ball to himself (a two-hand set, similar to a set in volleyball). A participant's score is the maximum number of sets completed without a miss.

VARIATIONS

- A group of swimmers must tread water and set the ball to each other. The score is the maximum number of passes done without the ball touching the water. In a group activity, everyone must set once before any swimmer can set a second time.
- Call an individual's name and require that person to receive the set. Count the number of sets within a given time.
- Add a penalty (such as swimming once around the group) for using only one hand.

KICKBOARD SCOOT

EQUIPMENT   One kickboard per person

DESCRIPTION   Each participant sits on a kickboard. Using only the arms or only the legs, the participant propels herself to the opposite side of the pool. Participants must maintain balance on the board throughout the activity.

VARIATIONS

- Require participants to carry a rolled-up towel in each hand or to wear water exercise gloves for increased resistance.
- For increased difficulty, require participants to use arm movements of the butterfly, front crawl, or back crawl (arm movements of the back crawl are done while moving backward).
- Place an object on the head of each participant. Add the rule that the participant cannot touch the object but must reach the other side of the pool without dropping the object.
- Vary the seated position. Ask participants to sit with legs extended straight out in front or crossed tailor-sit style.
- Have participants work in partners, sitting back to back, each on his own board. They must work together to accomplish the same task while maintaining back-to-back contact.
- Add blindfolds for each participant (and a safety spotter on deck).
- Have participants perform the activity seated on a water exercise noodle.

LAP CHASE TAG

EQUIPMENT   None

DESCRIPTION   Gather swimmers in one corner of the pool. The first swimmer starts swimming (in the first lane) to the opposite long end of the pool. When the first swimmer reaches a point approximately 12 yards out (six body lengths), the second swimmer follows the first. The object is for the second swimmer to catch and tag the foot of the first swimmer. Meanwhile, when the second swimmer is 12 yards out, the third swimmer starts. The third swimmer's task is to catch the second swimmer.

As successive swimmers start, they try to catch the swimmer immediately ahead. If a swimmer is successful in catching the swimmer ahead of him, the successful swimmer leaves the drill (without interfering with other swimmers). Everyone else continues to attempt to catch the swimmer swimming directly ahead of them. When one length is completed, the swimmer makes a U-turn into the next adjacent lane and continues swimming. As swimmers leave the drill, gaps open, and remaining swimmers have to work harder. Continue the drill until only two or three swimmers are left (and they are unable to catch each other). This is a good drill to use at the end of a class or workout. Early finishers can get a hot shower. If the drill is used at other times, early finishers can prepare equipment for other activities, or they can use a different area of the pool for practicing skills. This drill rewards maximum effort at the very start of the activity.

VARIATIONS

- Vary the swim order of participants. Initially, the strongest swimmer should go first to set a good pace. However, frequent rearrangement keeps swimmers' interest, giving each swimmer a renewed chance to catch someone.
- Vary the types of strokes used for the swim.
- Vary the distances between swimmers by having each one start on a signal rather than on distance.
- Have participants swim with rescue tubes in the approach position.

MUSICAL BRICKS

EQUIPMENT   10-pound brick; music source

DESCRIPTION   Swimmers tread water in a circle. When music plays, the brick is passed from swimmer to swimmer. When the music stops, the person holding the brick must drop it to the bottom. When the brick settles on the bottom, that same person must dive and retrieve it. When the brick is back up to the surface, the music starts again and swimmers continue to pass it.

VARIATIONS

- Vary the types of passes used (above water, one hand, two hand, above head).
- Expand the distance between swimmers.
- Have participants pass the brick to the beat of the music.
- Require participants to perform some other brick activity, such as Brick-Ups, between passes.
- Ask one swimmer to drop the brick, and the next swimmer to retrieve it. Another option is to have the swimmer who drops the brick call the name of any other swimmer, who must then retrieve the brick; participants then continue to pass from that new point.
- For added challenge, vary the weight of the brick used (5, 10, or 20 pounds).
- Have participants pass more than one brick at a time.

MUSICAL TUBES

EQUIPMENT   One or more rescue tubes; music source

DESCRIPTION   Participants tread water in a circle formation in deep water. Take one rescue tube and wrap the strap around the tube; secure the end so the strap does not drag. Then, start the music. As the music plays, participants pass the tube around the circle. When the music stops, the person in posses- sion of the tube must hold the tube over her head while the rest of the group sings a verse of a well-known song (such as "Row, Row, Row Your Boat" or "Jingle Bells"). When the singing is complete, the music is started again, and the participants continue to pass the tube.

VARIATIONS
- Require participants to keep the tube dry while passing. They must not allow the tube to touch the water.
- Require a specific type of pass (two hand, one hand with tube vertical, one hand with tube horizontal).
- Change the direction of passing.
- Have participants pass more than one tube at a time.
- If music is not available, substitute Brick-Ups, but use the tube instead of a brick.

Contributed by Sue Skaros, Milwaukee, WI

PASS IT ON

EQUIPMENT   A variety of different sized balls

DESCRIPTION   Swimmers tread water in a circle formation. One swimmer starts with a ball; this swimmer calls out the name of another swimmer and then passes the ball (above water) to that swimmer. The called swimmer catches the ball, calls another name, and passes the ball on to another player. Begin with one ball. Once all swimmers have made one pass, add a second ball, and then a third. Keep adding balls until there are almost as many balls as swimmers.

VARIATIONS

- Add a rule that no person can be called to receive a second pass until everyone in the group has received a pass. Or add a rule that no person can be called to receive a second pass of a particular ball until every swimmer has received that particular ball.
- Only allow three seconds for a person to catch a pass, call a name, and pass on.
- Specify a particular kick to be used while treading.
- Specify how high a pass must go (e.g., over the backstroke flags).
- Limit passes and catches to one hand only.

PFD SWAP

EQUIPMENT   One PFD (personal flotation device) for each team of six; one anchored buoy

DESCRIPTION   Divide participants into groups of six. Further divide each group of six in half, placing halves of each team on opposite sides of the deep end of the pool. Each group of three lines up single file with the first person in line directly opposite the first person in the corresponding group of three on the other side of the pool. A floating buoy is anchored equidistant from the two lines. One of the line leaders is wearing a PFD. On a predetermined signal, both line leaders water jog (they

do not swim) to the anchored buoy. On reaching the buoy, the person wearing the PFD must remove it and pass it to his counterpart from the opposite line. That person must put on the PFD. When the PFD is secured, both individuals high-five each other and then swim as quickly as possible back to their respective lines.

When the person wearing the PFD reaches his line, he takes off the device, gives it to the next person in line, and then goes to the end of the line. The person receiving the PFD must put it on and repeat the journey of the first person. The swimmer returning to his line without a PFD must tag the next swimmer and then go to the end of the line. In brief, the action is water jog out, swim return, then go to the end of the line. The activity is complete when the lines and the PFD are back in their starting arrangement. One team can repeat the activity, trying to better its own time, or several teams can race against each other.

VARIATIONS

- Have the first person in both lines wear a PFD. When they both reach the buoy, they must exchange PFDs and then return to their own lines.
- Add the wearing of clothing under the PFD. The person wearing the PFD must not only remove the PFD, but must also remove some additional article of clothing. The next person must then put on the article of clothing in addition to the PFD. The more clothing involved, the more difficult the task. Any clothing that is accidentally dropped to the bottom must be retrieved.
- Have one person wear the PFD and meet a person carrying a brick or other nonbuoyant object. They exchange both items.

Contributed by Sue Skaros, Milwaukee, WI

POLY TRAIL

EQUIPMENT   Medium and large Poly spots (15 to 25 spots total)

DESCRIPTION   Place a trail of Poly spots on the pool bottom. Each spot represents a stepping stone. Starting at one end of the trail, participants run or jump (depending on the placement of the spots) to the other end of the trail. On a single spot, the participant places one foot. If two spots are side by side, the participant jumps so that both feet land together on the spots. Vary the space between spots. Participants traverse the trail for speed, working to improve their time over their previous performance.

VARIATIONS

- Vary the distance or length of the trail. Or vary the water depth throughout the trail.
- Start a second person four seconds after the first person, and have the participants try to tag the person ahead of them.
- Vary the type of motor activity that must be done on each spot (i.e., hop on single spots, rather than stride or run).
- Combine the spots with aqua steps. Use the spots as a trail from aqua step to aqua step. On reaching each step, participants either step up and over the aqua step, or they stop at the step and perform step aerobics.
- Use the spots as a trail through a circuit training exercise course.
- Have participants traverse the trail moving backward.

PUSH ME PULL YOU

EQUIPMENT   One kickboard for every two participants

DESCRIPTION   Participants are grouped into pairs, and each pair is given a kickboard. The pairs then position themselves in two parallel lines in deep water, centered in the water area. Each set of partners has their kickboard between them. A lane line or other line marker is stretched behind each line; these markers should be as far back from the line as possible but at least a few feet from the nearest wall. For each pair of participants, one partner is assigned the letter *A*, and the other partner is assigned the letter *B*. Each partner grasps his end of the kickboard and treads water. The object of this activity is for one partner to either (1) push the opposite person back until that person's feet touch the lane line behind him or (2) pull the opposite person to the line behind the pulling person. On a predetermined signal and direction call—for example, "*A*s PUSH" or "*B*s PULL"—the action begins with the person whose letter is called performing the action specified. The opposite person (the one whose letter is not called) must offer resistance to the called action, becoming a drag for a pull or pushing back (through hard kicking) for a push.

Frequent signals and direction calls will reverse the action, creating turbulence and increasing the difficulty of the task. The task is completed when one person successfully pushes or pulls the opposite person to the appropriate line.

VARIATIONS
- Use rescue boards, and position the activity going the long way of the pool. Or use inner tubes or rescue tubes, which will be more difficult to grasp.
- Specify the kick to be used during the task.

Contributed by Carrie Paterson, Milwaukee, WI

SCOOP BALL CATCH

EQUIPMENT   One scoop ball set (large plastic scoops and one plastic ball) for each two participants. Scoop ball sets are readily available at a variety of discount stores, especially during the summer play season, and they can be found in the same department as other outdoor games and water toys.

DESCRIPTION   While treading water, partners play scoop ball. Scoops must be kept above water level. Players must catch the ball while it is in the air, and they must return it without letting it touch the water. Players count the number of successful catches made by the pair. The object is to make as many successful exchanges as possible.

VARIATIONS
- Vary the distance between players.
- Vary the number of players in the group by adding scoops to the equipment supply.
- Players can form groups of three and play keep away from the person in the middle.
- Substitute plastic badminton rackets and a birdie or ball, and see how many consecutive hits back and forth can be made without a miss.

SCOOP BALL PASS AROUND

EQUIPMENT One scoop ball scoop for each participant and one plastic ball for the group. Scoop ball sets are readily available at a variety of discount stores, especially during the summer play season, and they can be found in the same department as other outdoor games and water toys.

DESCRIPTION Participants tread water in a circle; each person holds his scoop above water. One person puts the ball into play by using his scoop and lofting the ball to the player opposite him in the circle.

That person must use his scoop to catch the ball and then throw it back—not to the person who threw to him, but to the person to the left of that person in the circle. Exchanges continue back and forth with each person throwing the ball to the next person to the left of the person who threw to him. In this manner, the ball moves completely around the circle.

VARIATIONS

- Time how long it takes the group to successfully move the ball completely around the circle. Have the group repeat the activity to better its time.
- Put more than one ball into play at a time. Have participants move two or more balls around in opposite directions.
- Substitute plastic badminton rackets and a birdie for the scoop ball equipment.

SHOOTER SHOOT

EQUIPMENT   Space shooter. A space shooter is an inflatable tube that is 4 feet (122 cm) long and about the diameter of a rescue tube. If a space shooter is not available, a giant noodle (full size or half size) may be used for this activity. Noodles come in several circumferences and lengths. A noodle with a solid core and larger circumference will fly better than one that is hollow and narrow and hence more flexible.

DESCRIPTION   Swimmers line up in deep water, forming two parallel lines on opposite sides of the pool. Lines are one lane away from the sides of the pool. A center line is marked, either with a lane line or cones on the deck. No swimmer may cross the center line. Swimmers tread water with their backs to the side of the pool. The object is to shoot the space shooter over the reach of the opposing team and onto the opposite pool deck. Players try to block incoming shots, and they try to catch the space shooter for their own goal tries. The wider the distance between the sides of the pool, the more difficult this task will be. If a shot is blocked, the blocking team has possession and can try for their opponent's deck. Points are given for successful deck landings. Players defending a shot may not touch the side of the pool.

VARIATIONS

- For greater challenge, have more than one space shooter going at one time.
- Vary the object used as the shooter. Because of its unusual shape, a space shooter is designed to fly but is difficult to catch. Substituted objects should fly reasonably well but should not hurt a person's hands during a block or catch.

SIMON SAYS

EQUIPMENT None

DESCRIPTION Swimmers tread water (they may use their arms). A leader chosen from the group gives commands to the group, specifying a motor activity to be done while treading. Commands may be preceded by the introduction "Simon says." If Simon says to do something, everyone in the group must do it. If a command is given without "Simon says," no one should do the activity.

An incorrect response by a member of the group should result in a penalty (not in being out of the activity). The penalty might be 10 push-ups on the edge of the pool, 10 bottom bobs, or a somersault. Leadership should rotate around the whole group. Change leaders every five commands (this may vary depending on the size of the group).

VARIATIONS Add hand equipment. Give each participant the same type of hand equipment, such as hand mitts, aqua barbells, or bricks.

SWIM THE WORLD

EQUIPMENT Destination map posted on a bulletin board or taped to a pool wall; fine-point Magic Markers in a variety of colors

DESCRIPTION Swimmers review the map and select a swim destination. The object is to swim the distance required to get from the city of the swimmers' home pool to their selected destination. Laps are counted in miles. Depending on the scale of the map, miles are traced on the map with Magic Marker. With a small group of swimmers, each swimmer can select her own destination and have her own color for map tracing. Having different destinations for each individual works best for city and in-state destinations.

A large group of swimmers might want to divide into two or three teams; all teams head for the same destination, and they see which team can arrive first. Or the whole group can work together to achieve a swim to a European or Asian destination. Swimmers swim during their free water time, logging mileage on the map with Magic Markers as they complete the distances.

VARIATIONS For longer-distance destinations, swimmers may need to keep track of miles on a simple count chart or list, transferring markings to a map in 10- or 20-mile segments. Teams of individuals will cover more mileage than individual swimmers. Accomplishment cards can be given for mileage segments. Teams can race against each other to swim to the same destination. This activity can also be done mimicking traditional long-distance swims, such as swimming the English Channel. Groups of students can compete with each other to see who can reach a specific destination first. A swim destination can be combined with a fund-raising activity for an extended group event.

TOWEL SWIM

EQUIPMENT Two towels for each swimmer

DESCRIPTION Roll a standard athletic towel into a roll so it can be held in one hand. Swimmers swim a front crawl with a towel in each hand. Stress that swimmers should bend the elbow properly on recovery and should pull down under the midline of the body.

VARIATIONS

- Vary the size of the towel depending on the size of the swimmer's hand. The towel should not drag in the water; rather, it should be compact and held so it comes completely out of the water during arm recovery.
- Vary the fabric of the towel. Thin towels weigh less than large fluffy ones.
- Have participants use the towels while treading water in a stationary position. Swimmers must keep the towels above water while treading. Additional arm exercises above water can be added for increased difficulty.

TRAVEL TREAD

EQUIPMENT   None

DESCRIPTION   While treading water, swimmers move through an obstacle course on the surface of the water. The course might be verbal—for example, verbal commands are given to move forward three body lengths in lane 1, backward one body length in lane 2, circle spin right, backward to the end of lane 2, sideward right slide tread in lane 3, and left circle spin traveling back to the start. The course could also be set up with floating objects that swimmers must navigate through without touching. Be sure participants remain upright—in treading position—rather than lean forward toward horizontal swimming.

VARIATIONS

- Time the participants' performance through the obstacle course.
- Have participants use only their arms for treading, keeping their legs still, straight, and together or tucked up knees to chest.
- Substitute lengths of Travel Tread for stroke swimming during a lap swim. While participants are in deep water, Travel Tread is used. When participants reach shallow water, they run (they do not swim).
- Have participants perform Travel Tread activities moving backward.
- Conduct relay races using the Travel Tread.

TUBE SIT RACE

EQUIPMENT   One rescue tube per person (or per team)

DESCRIPTION   Each participant sits in a straddle position over his rescue tube. Participants race over a given distance using the arm movements of the front crawl, back crawl, breaststroke, butterfly, or sculling. The direction of travel can be forward, backward, or spinning.

VARIATIONS

- Make this a two-part race. Participants swim out to a marker while towing the tube, as if making a rescue. At the destination, they sit on the tube and race back as described.
- Conduct the race as a relay.
- Add a blindfold that the participating relay member must wear, forcing the other team members to provide verbal guidance.
- Add retrieval of an object to the race. The task becomes swim out, retrieve the object, and then race back carrying the object and bicycling while sitting on the tube.

TUG-OF-WAR

EQUIPMENT   A length of rope at least 6 feet (183 cm) long with a center mark and hand loops on each end

DESCRIPTION   A starter holds the center mark of the rope in the center of the swim area, preferably the center of deep water. One swimmer at each end holds the end loop of the rope. Caution: Swimmers should not put the loop of the rope around their wrist. Check the length of the rope before starting. When the pull begins, swimmers will be swimming away from each other; therefore, their feet and legs should not touch during the rope check. On "go," swimmers swim in opposite directions. The first swimmer to reach her side of the pool (or a designated goal point) is the winner. The sidestroke is usually the most productive stroke to swim for this race.

VARIATIONS

- Give each swimmer a rescue tube. Swimmers position on their backs with arms forward over the rescue tube to grasp the rope with both hands. Conduct the pull with participants swimming on their backs.

- Have participants perform this activity dressed (as for the Clothes Swim described earlier in this chapter).

- Have swimmers position on their backs and kick with the inverted breast-stroke kick during the pull.

- Make this a partner or team event. If space is available for a longer rope to be laid out, make additional loops in the rope a sufficient distance apart so that swimmers holding those loops will not kick each other. Then add a participant for each loop. Caution: Loops that are too close together will cause swimmers to kick teammates and cause injury.

TWO ON A TUBE TUG

EQUIPMENT   Two rescue tubes for every four participants

DESCRIPTION   Participants are divided into teams of two. Each two-person team has one rescue tube. Each team takes a seated (straddle) position on their rescue tube; the strap end of the tube should be extended out in front of the forward seated person. Once seated on their tube, each pair hand-paddles until facing another tube pair. When two pairs are facing each other, the front person on each tube reaches out and grasps the tube strap of the opposite tube. On a predetermined signal, each pair tries to pull their opponents' tube out from under them.

Hands may be used for paddling or for holding a tube strap. However, hands may not touch either tube. Legs may be used to paddle (kick) or wrap around the tube. However, legs may not be used on the tube strap. The first team to unseat their opponent wins.

VARIATIONS

- Rather than strive to unseat opponents, partners can attempt to pull their opponent a predetermined distance. The first team to accomplish the pull is the winner.
- Another person can be added to each tube, making teams of three or four.

VOLLEY

EQUIPMENT Equipment will vary depending on the type of volley task performed.

DESCRIPTION A volley involves two individuals exchanging a small item of equipment by applying a force to that equipment. In volleyball, individuals volley a ball back and forth. In badminton, participants volley a badminton birdie. Volleying performed in an aquatic environment can also be a good conditioning activity for lifeguards. For conditioning, the volley should be performed in deep water. This will force participants to tread. Depending on whether one hand or two are used for the volley, participants may also be able to scull for support.

Here are some typical volley activities appropriate for in-water conditioning:

- Volleying a ball (as in volleyball)
- Volleying a beach ball in the same manner as volleying a ball
- Using plastic paddles to volley a plastic badminton birdie
- Using plastic paddles to volley a Wiffle ball (as in tennis)

Two individuals can volley back and forth, counting each hit. When a miss occurs, the count must go back to zero. Pairs can repeatedly try to better their own score, or they can try to beat the highest score by another pair in the group.

VARIATIONS

- Increase the distance between the two people volleying.
- Add a rope line or net that the object must be volleyed over.
- Add a time factor. Participants see how many volleys they can complete during a specific amount of time, or they see how quickly they can perform a set number of volleys.
- Have each pair start a volley and then travel the length of the pool while maintaining the volley. Specify the stroke that participants must use while swimming and volleying.

WALK A LAP

EQUIPMENT   None

DESCRIPTION   Participants start at the shallow end of the pool. Taking giant strides, participants walk all the way to the other end. When the drop-off is reached, participants continue the long stride, even though their feet will not touch bottom. Participants' heads must remain above water at all times. No other leg action is allowed. Hands may be placed in any nonuse position.

VARIATIONS   To increase difficulty, require participants to perform the activity with arms overhead, while carrying a brick at water level, or while fully clothed.

WATER POLO

EQUIPMENT   Balls that are the appropriate size for water polo (one ball for each participant)

DESCRIPTION   The sport of water polo can provide a variety of conditioning activities for lifeguard training. Because water polo relies heavily on treading water, as well as strong swimming ability, this sport is an excellent conditioning activity. Specific water polo activities include the following:

- Dribbling the ball. The swimmer swims the front crawl with the ball in front of the head and between the arms. The ball may not be carried. Rather, it must be pushed forward by the momentum of the swimmer.
- Passing and catching. The swimmer passes the ball to another participant using a one-hand underhand toss. The receiver either catches the ball with one hand or lets it land in the water. The ball may not be carried after a catch.

- Blocking a shot. The participant uses a strong, vertically propulsive tread to rise as high out of the water as possible, using a hand to block or deflect a pass or shot of an opponent.

The following are appropriate drill applications for water polo skills:

- Two participants, spaced at least a body length apart, must pass the ball back and forth as they swim a length of the pool.
- Two participants, spaced at least a body length apart, must pass the ball back and forth as they swim a length of the pool. A third person swims between them, trying to block the pass. If the pass is successfully blocked, the center person becomes a passing swimmer, and the passing swimmer becomes the center person.

- Participants are divided into teams. Each team selects a goalie, who is stationed treading at one end of the pool. The team lines up at the opposite end (single file). The first person must dribble out to a specific point and then pass to his goalie. To further challenge participants, place a member of another team to act as interference for the shooter. If the pass is deflected, the opponents get a point. If the pass is successful, the passing team scores. After a single shot, the goalie dribbles back to the line, and the shooter becomes goalie.
- The ball dribble can be used in any type of relay race.

VARIATIONS   Numerous resources are available to help you find additional water polo activities. Integrating water polo into lifeguard training will bring many strength, endurance, and cardiorespiratory benefits. In addition, it will introduce your lifeguards to another aquatic activity for participation and enjoyment.

WEIGHTED TREAD

EQUIPMENT A set of ankle weights, a weight belt, or wrist weights

DESCRIPTION Participants wear a weight belt, ankle weights, or wrist weights while treading (they may use any combination of this equipment). Participants should gradually increase the weight as their leg strength increases. They may also wear the weight belt while swimming. This additional weight provides many strength-building benefits. In addition, for individuals who are extremely buoyant, adding weight can assist them in maneuvering their body under water. This is particularly useful for people who have extreme difficulty in completing a feetfirst surface dive.

VARIATIONS

- Rolled-up towels held in the hand can be substituted for wrist weights.
- Swimmers can combine ankle weights, weight belt, and handheld towels for a full-weight workout.
- This activity may also be combined with the Clothes Swim (see page 33).

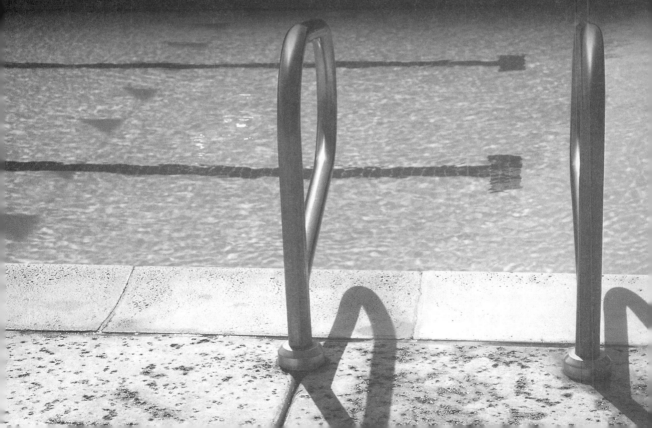

3

Safety, Surveillance, and Scanning Activities

Not all lifeguarding skills are physical. Successful performance as a lifeguard also requires cognitive skills and abilities. These skills and abilities include the following:

- Recognizing and understanding the components of a safe environment for aquatic participation
- Being able to establish and maintain a safe environment for aquatic participation
- Self-governing personal behavior in order to be a role model for safe aquatic participation
- Performing appropriate patron surveillance 100 percent of the time on duty
- Scanning with 100 percent accuracy in identifying the safety status of swimmers
- Scanning with appropriate timing and repetition of the scanning process
- Translating victim recognition into a safe and appropriate response to any emergent situation

For a lifeguard, safety means more than being a safe participant. As an aquatic professional, a lifeguard must be able to generate safe participant behavior in others. This requires lifeguards to be proficient in the following tasks:

- Establishing rules for safe participant behavior.
- Communicating these rules to participants of a variety of ages, abilities, comprehension levels, and motivations.
- Enforcing compliance with the rules of the aquatic facility where the lifeguard is employed.
- Establishing a safe aquatic environment before opening the facility to participants. This includes overseeing facility equipment, as well as maintenance operations.
- Evaluating the safety status of the facility throughout the lifeguard's on-duty hours.
- Proficiently using all equipment available at the facility.
- Recognizing any need for change or improvement in any aspect of safe facility operations—and being able to act to implement those changes.

Surveillance is the big-picture aspect of the job of the lifeguard. It requires the constant ability to see the circumstances present in the aquatic environment, as well as the ability to process information and make decisions. Surveillance includes the following:

- Maintaining the mental focus to constantly evaluate what is seen in comparison with a mental picture of a safe participant in a safe aquatic environment
- Recognizing any and every deviation from the norm of safe aquatic participation
- Selecting the appropriate personal response to any unsafe behavior
- Performing the scanning process effectively

Scanning refers to repeated viewing of a select visual field, with ongoing evaluation of what is seen. Here are some of the requirements for effective scanning:

- Having knowledge of the exact boundaries of the area to be scanned
- Establishing an ocular tracking pattern to cover the prescribed scan area in an efficient period of time
- Repeating the ocular tracking pattern an untold number of times without a break in the pattern and without a loss of mental focus; this must include the ongoing processing of visual information
- Sorting information obtained from the scan to identify types of behavior and to isolate safe behavior from behavior that requires a response
- Immediately translating information processed from the visual scan into the appropriate motor activity for a successful response to any emergency

These are the components of the activities and games in this chapter. Safety, surveillance, and scanning are largely cognitive in nature. As noted previously, not all strong swimmers have equally strong cognitive abilities or information-processing abilities. Activities and games can provide reinforcement for text learning, as well as opportunities to apply learned information in situations that are similar to actual emergencies.

In addition, it is difficult to assess the practical application of a cognitive skill. A written test can provide information on how well a person understands the concepts involved in safety, surveillance, and scanning. However, no written test can assess the person's actual application of these concepts. Activities and games can be used to assess learned knowledge through practical application. The activities and games in this chapter lend themselves well to partner and group training, as well as individual participation and reinforcement. They can be implemented as part of a class or as homework. If your program includes a Web site, many of these activities can also be adapted to online education.

COLOR SCAN

EQUIPMENT   10 to 15 Poly spots of various colors; a watch with a second hand

DESCRIPTION   Determine a specific zone for a lifeguard position, and decide how many seconds a lifeguard should take to scan the entire area one time. Then, blindfold the participant so he cannot see the placement of equipment. Place the Poly spots in a relatively straight line across the entire area (or zone) that

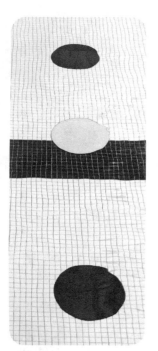

the lifeguard should scan in the determined time. Place the lifeguard in his guard position. On a predetermined signal, start the time, and have the lifeguard remove his blindfold. The lifeguard immediately begins scanning his zone. While scanning, the lifeguard should call out the colors of the Poly spots as each is encountered during the scan.

When the established time limit has been reached, call "stop." The lifeguard should stop scanning at that point. Note how many colors the lifeguard called correctly, as well as how many colors were not called or were called incorrectly. Subtract the number of colors missed (uncalled or incorrectly called) from the number that the lifeguard called correctly—this determines the individual's score. Then blindfold the lifeguard again, set up a different color sequence, and repeat the activity. Each time the lifeguard repeats the activity, he should strive for a higher score by scanning more quickly and with greater accuracy. If a lifeguard completes an entire scan sweep before time is called, the lifeguard should reverse the scan direction and continue calling colors until time is stopped.

VARIATIONS

- Vary the sizes of the Poly spots (they come in a variety of sizes), and have the lifeguard call size in addition to color. Poly equipment also comes in shark and frog shapes. Add these to the mix, and have the lifeguard call color, size, and shape.
- Vary the size and configuration of the zone to be covered.
- Add floating objects on the surface of the water; these objects make the activity more challenging by obstructing the view of the lifeguard.

FLASH CARD VICTIMS

EQUIPMENT   One set of victim flash cards. Victim flash cards are made by taking digital photographs of swimmers of a variety of ages in a variety of positions. Here are some examples of what may be shown on these cards:

- Swimmers performing normal swimming (variety of strokes)
- Swimmers performing underwater swimming
- Swimmers playing a game
- Swimmer bobbing into water that just covers the nose and mouth
- Tired swimmer
- Swimmer struggling just below the surface in deep water
- Swimmer struggling just below the surface next to the wall
- Swimmer treading water
- Unresponsive swimmer on the surface, face up
- Unresponsive swimmer on the surface, face down
- Unresponsive swimmer below the surface, but not on the bottom
- Unresponsive swimmer on the bottom
- Swimmer standing in shallow water, with a grimace on his face, and clutching his chest
- Swimmer (in shallow water) who has lost balance and is unable to regain footing

Take the photos with volunteer models playing the roles. Be sure to shoot the pictures during regular open swims at your facility. Photos should look similar to what a lifeguard would see during a scan. Once the photos have been taken, turn each photo into a flash card by printing the photo onto card stock paper. On the back of the flash card photo, write "OK" if the swimmer appears in no danger. Also add a short description of what the swimmer is doing (such as "surface diving"). Write "RESCUE" if the swimmer appears in need of rescue, and include a brief description of why a rescue is needed (such as "head injury from collision").

DESCRIPTION   Flash the victim flash cards to the lifeguard, allowing only a brief look (1 or 2 seconds). As each card is flashed, the lifeguard must call out the type of swimmer. The lifeguard calls out "OK" if the card shows a swimmer who is not in need of assistance. The lifeguard calls out "RESCUE" if the card shows a victim in need of assistance. Keep a tally of how many victim identifications the lifeguard gets correct. Review victim characteristics of any victims identified incorrectly.

...continued

VARIATIONS

- Divide the group into teams. Have teams compete to make the first correct identification of each victim.

- Expand the contents of the flash cards to include pool rules being broken (and thus needing lifeguard intervention), facility management situations (such as cleanliness and equipment checks), and skill performance cards (where viewers have to decide if the skill shown is being performed correctly or incorrectly). Flash cards can also be used by individuals as a home study option.

- Vary the activity by putting the digital photos into a slide show program such as PowerPoint. Participants view the slide show and try to correctly identify the status of the swimmers. The changing photos are presented in increasingly quick succession, so participants will also see how fast they can accurately identify swimmer status. Flash Card Victims can also be set up as an online activity, enabling lifeguards to perform the activity from home (as an aspect of in-service training).

GUARD ARRANGEMENT

EQUIPMENT   Pictures of a variety of swimming pools; paper and pencils

DESCRIPTION   Each participant is given a picture of a different pool. In writing, participants must complete the following tasks for the pool they are given:

- Post positions for lifeguard stations, stating whether each is a stand or a walking guard location.
- Define zones of surveillance for each guard position.
- List pool rules.
- List and place the safety and rescue equipment needed at the pool.
- List and place safety signage.
- List activities that are appropriate for the pool, indicating what types of programs could safely be offered there.
- List activities that are inappropriate for the pool, indicating what types of programs should not be staged there.

Each participant should exchange all information with another participant; partners then evaluate each other's information for safety and practicality. Have participants orally present their final results to the entire group, checking off items on the assignment as each is covered. Discuss any areas of controversy or concern.

VARIATIONS

- Present the activity as homework. At the next session, have participants exchange pool designs so they can do the evaluations as homework.
- To encourage participants to work together, assign this project to teams, rather than individuals.

LOCATE AND RETRIEVE

EQUIPMENT   Eight pairs of sweatpants

DESCRIPTION   This activity takes place during a regular open swim. Eight individuals are wearing sweatpants over their swimsuits, and they are swimming and playing with the rest of the participants at the open swim. Regular lifeguards are on duty. In addition, one lifeguard—the lifeguard participating in this activity—performs appropriate scanning at one of the guard positions.

Another person (the activity monitor) is positioned on deck with a stopwatch. Several minutes into the swim period, one of the swimmers wearing sweatpants quickly and unobtrusively allows her sweatpants to drop off and sink to the bottom. This person then continues swimming as if nothing has happened. As soon as the sweatpants drop, the monitor starts the stopwatch. The monitor times how long it takes for the participating lifeguard to notice the downed trousers, activate the EAP by signaling and calling out, "Drill in progress," and retrieve the sweatpants. Time stops when the pants are placed on the deck. Note: The monitor should know which individual is going to drop the pants so that time is started promptly. The more people in the pool during the open swim, the more difficult the completion of this activity will be—from the standpoint of scanning and recognition, as well as retrieval.

VARIATIONS   Vary the color or size of the sweatpants. Darker colors are easier to see against a pool bottom. Larger pants are easier to see and retrieve.

PASS THE MESSAGE

EQUIPMENT   None

DESCRIPTION   Participants are stationed around the pool at positions that would be typical lifeguard stations. Seated guards may sit. Standing guards may stand. One additional participant starts this activity by walking in from the side and going to the closest guard station. On reaching the station, the arriving guard gives the guard on station a spoken message. After the delivery of the message, the arriving guard and the on-station guard must correctly change places. Once the exchange has been done, the guard who is now "free" walks to the next guard station; on arrival, the guard passes the same message to the next guard.

Again, after the delivery of the message, the two guards perform an appropriate change of position, and the new free guard takes the message onward. The activity is complete when the message reaches the first person (the person who started the message). This person confirms the accuracy of the message and indicates how well executed each of the exchanges appeared to be. The exchanges should be evaluated on correct movement of guards, unbroken surveillance during the message, and proper exchange of place.

VARIATIONS

- Vary the length of the message. Begin with a simple sentence. Expand the content to several sentences.
- Let each guard in the sequence add to the first sentence of the message, similar to making up a story.
- Add an interruption to the focus of the guard moving from station to station. This might be someone coming to talk to the guard, or it could be a noise or distraction in the pool. Discuss with the participants how distractions interfere with mental focus as well as performance of physical tasks.

POOL DESIGN

EQUIPMENT   Paper and pencil

DESCRIPTION   After studying aquatic facility safety, lifeguards are asked to design the safest pool imaginable. Money is no object. Evaluate participants' designs based on a number of safety features that should be included. In evaluating designs, look for the following:

Depth markings	Rescue tubes
Lifelines	Signage for pool rules
Diving area	Nonskid deck
Chemical testing equipment	Lane line rollers
Posted emergency numbers	Guard stands
Reach poles	Ladders
First aid supplies and AED	Safe chemical storage
Fence (outdoor)	Underwater motion sensors and monitoring equipment
Stair railings	Underwater camera system and monitoring equipment
Posted EAP	
Ring buoys	Above-water camera system and monitoring equipment
Phone	
Door locks	Spectator area
Equipment storage	Local ordinance requirements

VARIATIONS

- Have participants define the purpose of the pool before they create the design. Include home pools as well as community (recreational), school, and club (competitive) pools. Participants can specify activities that should be able to be staged in the pool. For example, synchronized swimming needs deeper water, as does springboard diving.
- Ask designers to also mark zone coverage areas for lifeguards.
- Ask participants to score each other's pools.
- Have participants add written rules for the designed pools.
- If water park lifeguarding is included, ask participants to design a water park venue.

POSTER DESIGN

EQUIPMENT   Large sheets of paper, color Magic Markers, old magazines, scissors, and glue or tape

DESCRIPTION   Every aquatic facility will experience problems at some point. This might range from general litter to a particular pool rule that children repeatedly break. Lifeguards should be involved in problem solving, rather than just correction of patrons. A proactive role gives your lifeguards ownership in your well-run facility. Ask your lifeguards to describe one or two problems that they think persist among your patron group. Brainstorm with the lifeguards to determine which problems are most prevalent, annoying, or unsafe. Then, ask your lifeguards to design posters to spread information that will help correct the problem. Stress that the posters should focus on the positive—what patrons should be doing and why they should be doing it. Posters can be colorful collages or stark printed data. Your lifeguards know your clients best. When the posters are finished, display them in appropriate areas of your facility. Posters will be interesting additions, and they will be noticeable to patrons—if only because a poster will be different from what the patrons usually see. Sometimes patrons ignore safety postings just because the sign has always been there, but the patron never really read it. A new poster is a different way to focus attention. If you are placing a poster where it will get wet, cover it with plastic or laminate it to protect against water damage. Caution: A poster should not take the place of (nor cover up) existing safety signage.

VARIATIONS
- Expand this activity to be a competition for poster of the month. Ask patrons to vote on best poster, and display winning posters in the lobby or on bulletin boards throughout the facility.
- Present the activity as something a lifeguard can do at home.
- Provide additional incentives for creative results. This might be an additional hour's pay, time off, a longer break, or having the best poster put on a T-shirt or button.

SAFETY CHECK

EQUIPMENT   A full complement of standard pool equipment for your facility; copies of your facility's preopening safety checklist (one copy for each participant); pencils

DESCRIPTION   This activity enables participants to practice conducting a preopening safety check. Before participants enter the pool area and locker room to begin this activity, you will need to arrange the pool so that the safety check is challenging. It is very easy to conduct a preopening check when a facility is in perfect order. To make a practice check useful, you must create some disorder. Changes should be subtle; they should also be the type of changes that would result from facility use and programming. Here are some typical changes that might be made in order to create disorder:

- Spilled coffee or soda in the locker room
- Kickboards left on the deck
- Dirt on the deck
- No toilet paper in bathrooms
- Lifeline coiled on deck
- Rescue tubes not at guard stands
- Incomplete supplies in first aid kit
- AED or oxygen not in correct location
- Phone out of order (unplugged)
- Chemical balance of pool water not in compliance (substitute placebo for test chemicals to get inaccurate reading)
- Rescue equipment missing

Once the changes have been made to create disorder, give a checklist to each participant. Admit the participants to the facility so they can perform the preopening check. Each participant should complete his checklist without conferring with any other participant. When everyone is finished, compare the results of each participant's check with the items of disorder you created. For each item of disorder found by the participants, you should discuss what must be done before the pool can be opened. Remember that participants may also find items needing correction that were not part of the disorder you purposely caused. Be prepared to accept all input that can help improve the safety of facility users.

VARIATIONS   This activity may also be used to practice completing a pool closing checklist. At the end of each day of facility use, lifeguard staff should ensure that the facility is left in a condition to be efficiently opened by the next day's staff. Although cleaning will likely be done in the interim, lifeguards should perform certain tasks before leaving for the day. These tasks should be included on a pool closing checklist. Here are some of the items that should be included on this checklist:

- Decks are clear of all equipment used by participants.
- Equipment used by participants is placed in appropriate storage areas.
- Rescue equipment is racked or stored appropriately.
- First aid supplies expended during the day or shift have been replaced.
- AED and oxygen are in place and secure.
- Repairs needed or requests for special cleaning have been noted for maintenance personnel.
- Water quality has been checked, and pool chemicals are secured.

SAFETY CONCENTRATION

EQUIPMENT   One set of Safety Concentration cards. To make Safety Concentration cards, first compile a list of matching items, such as the following:

- Victim symptom and appropriate first aid—for example, moderate bleeding and direct pressure
- Type of victim and appropriate rescue—for example, a victim who dove into shallow water and a rescue using backboarding
- Type of victim and victim characteristic—for example, a tired swimmer and the characteristic of swimming slowly, with a weak kick

Then print out the list and cut the list into individual pieces so that each piece of paper contains one word or phrase from a pair of matching items. If you printed the words and phrases onto card stock paper, you can use them as they are. If you printed on regular paper, glue the words onto heavier paper or onto old playing cards, creating a Safety Concentration deck of cards. Each card should be blank on one side and should have the safety word or phrase on the other side.

DESCRIPTION   Mix the cards and lay them out printed side down in multiple rows. Ask the first participant to turn over two random cards as shown in the illustration. Obviously, "No pulse" and "Splint" do not match. When no match occurs, both cards are turned back over, and it becomes the next participant's turn. Each person attempts to turn over two cards that match each other, as in the game Concentration. When a person turns over two cards that match, those cards are removed from the table, and two points are awarded to the person who made the match. The game continues until all cards have been matched and removed.

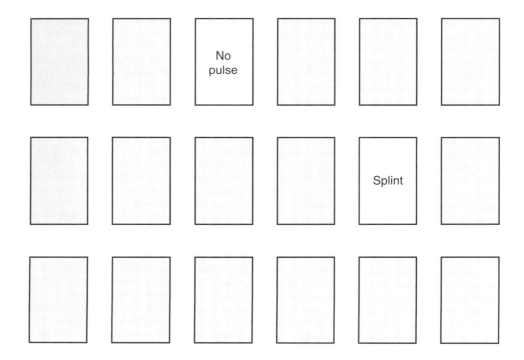

VARIATIONS

- Design three-part categories and require three cards to be turned over on each turn. For example, the three categories could include a first aid situation (e.g., hypothermia), a symptom (e.g., blue skin), and the appropriate first aid (e.g., rewarm slowly).
- Add a time limit for card selection, such as forcing participants to select the second card within three seconds. This encourages quick thinking.
- Use pictures for one half of a matching pair. For example, a picture of a victim on the pool bottom could be matched with "submerged victim rescue."

SAFETY DAY

SAFETY DAY

EQUIPMENT Equipment will vary based on the safety skills being taught or demonstrated. The equipment needed might include essential rescue equipment, small craft, water toys, clothing, or inflatables.

DESCRIPTION Every aquatic program should have a commitment to aquatic safety. Hosting a Safety Day turns that commitment into actual practice by taking the safety initiative to the program participants. A Safety Day highlights personal safety in and around the water. This event may include the following:

- Short classes (15 to 30 minutes in length) on safety skills, such as rescues performed by reaching, how to help a victim of conscious choking, or safe participation in the sun
- Demonstrations of safety skills, such as self-rescue or what to do when a small craft capsizes
- Posters and take-home flyers promoting safety issues, such as learning how to swim or swimming with a buddy
- Longer classes (1 to 2 hours) teaching a safety concept in greater depth, such as home pool safety or CPR
- Small safety lessons taught within other aquatic program classes, such as how to release a cramp or how to perform a survival float

Lifeguards are great teachers for Safety Day activities. Teaching or leading events on Safety Day enables lifeguards to have personal interaction with program participants. For children, the lifeguard can become more than an enforcer of rules. For adults, the lifeguard can become more than the person in the guard chair. As a Safety Day teacher, the lifeguard becomes a safety ambassador, as well as a public relations spokesperson for your program. In addition, the lifeguards reinforce their own personal safety and rescue skills while teaching them to others.

VARIATIONS This activity is as varied as the events included in the Safety Day schedule. A lifeguard who is new to Safety Day teaching can team-teach with a more experienced guard. Junior guards can demonstrate techniques or serve as victims for demonstrations by other lifeguards. Safety Day can be an event covered by a local news agency, providing good advertising for your program.

SCAN TEST

EQUIPMENT   Digital camera; a pool diagram on paper; pencil

DESCRIPTION   This activity takes place during a regular open swim. All on-duty lifeguards are in their usual positions, and the open swim proceeds normally. The person performing the Scan Test takes a position next to one of the on-duty lifeguards; this person stands with her back to the water. A person with a digital camera takes a position facing the testing guard.

On a signal, the testing guard turns, faces the pool, and performs a four- or five-second scan of the area of responsibility she would have if working that guard station. After the scan, the testing guard turns back to face the cameraperson. During the scan, the cameraperson takes a digital photo (over the shoulder of the testing guard) of the area being scanned. After the scan is done, the testing guard takes the pool diagram (and pencil) and makes arrows and Xs on the diagram to indicate swimmers seen during the scan. After the guard completes the diagram, the diagram is compared with the photo for accuracy. When comparing the diagram with the photo, look for accuracy in the number of swimmers, the direction of swimmer travel, and complete coverage of the scanned area.

VARIATIONS

- Ask certain swimmers to perform specific tasks during the scan—for example, underwater swimming, surface diving, and entering or exiting the water.
- Ask the testing guard for a more specific identification of swimmers, such as red suit or blue cap.

SCRAMBLED SEQUENCES

EQUIPMENT   Safety sequence cards. These cards represent the sequence of steps in a particular safety procedure. To make safety sequence cards, you first need to determine what knowledge and skills must be learned in order to perform the applicable safety procedure. Here are some typical procedures that safety sequence cards may be created to represent:

- Performing a primary survey
- Performing first aid for a choking victim, a choking victim who is unresponsive, a nonbreathing victim, or a victim without a pulse
- Assembling an AED
- Assembling an oxygen tank
- Placing a victim on a backboard
- Performing a rescue for a victim with a spinal cord injury
- Performing a rescue for a submerged victim
- Performing the procedure for lifeguards changing positions

Once you have determined the skills and knowledge included in the procedure, you should list these items of skill and knowledge in the appropriate sequence. After making the list, print each item on a three-by-five-inch card. For example, a set of sequence cards for a primary survey would look like this:

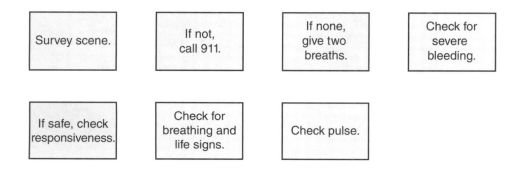

On the back of each card, write the number that represents the card's place in the sequence.

DESCRIPTION   For each safety procedure, mix the printed cards.

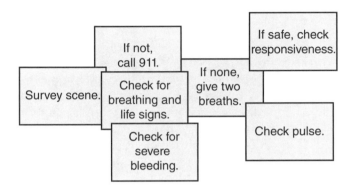

Once the cards are mixed, ask the participant to place the cards in the correct order.

Verify the final placement by checking the numbers on the backs of the cards. Correct any incorrect sequences, and have the participant try again.

VARIATIONS

- Take digital photos of a person performing the sequences. Then make sequence cards from the photos, rather than use printed words. Another option is to use a mix of photos and printed cards.
- To further challenge the participant, add a card or two into the mix that have nothing to do with the applicable safety procedure.

Survey scene.

If safe, check responsiveness.

If not, call 911.

Check for breathing and life signs.

If none, give two breaths.

Check pulse.

Check for severe bleeding.

TEACH ONE

EQUIPMENT Equipment will vary based on the safety skills being taught. The equipment needed might include a towel, PFD, pole, or rescue tube.

DESCRIPTION One of the best ways for people to reinforce their learning of knowledge or skills is to teach that knowledge or skill to another person or persons. Lifeguards are continually faced with the challenge of helping participants maintain safe behavior in and around the water. This often includes having to actually teach safety skills. Being a lifeguard means more than just telling a patron to stop doing something. Appropriate lifeguarding means telling patrons what they SHOULD be doing. This is teaching. Lifeguards need just as much practice teaching as they do performing other job-related tasks. Here are some of the reasons that teaching is an important skill for lifeguards:

- Teaching helps a lifeguard learn to communicate with patrons, and it "breaks the ice" in patron contact.
- Teaching helps a lifeguard develop efficient language for stating what he wants to say in a brief, yet clear, manner.
- Teaching gives a lifeguard a view into the mind of the participant, as participants ask questions or make comments during the teaching process.
- Teaching presents the lifeguard in a friendly light, thus making the lifeguard seem more approachable if a patron needs assistance in the future.
- Teaching establishes a future standard of behavior for participants.
- Teaching places the lifeguard in the role of knowledgeable professional, which adds to his self-esteem and confidence.
- Teaching is a recruitment tool—when lifeguards are seen in leadership roles, younger swimmers may strive to become the lifeguard they see teaching.

Lifeguards have many opportunities for teaching. These opportunities might include the following:

- Reaching out to give safety presentations at local schools and community centers. This is particularly important in areas where aquatic participation may be seasonal.
- Providing safety orientation to groups before pool parties and other group events.
- Leading Safety Day activities at the facility. (Refer to Safety Day [see page 82] for further information.)
- Resolving an altercation between patrons, especially children.
- Providing instruction on safety skills during learn-to-swim classes.
- Providing special interest workshops for the community at large (e.g., a workshop on backyard pool safety or a workshop on safe boating during fishing season).
- Acting as a teaching assistant in lifeguard training classes.

Here are some examples of the topics that are appropriate for lifeguards to teach:

- Personal safety around water
- How to perform reaching rescues
- How to use a PFD
- Safety in the sun (sunburn and heat-related illnesses)
- Winter water safety
- Safe behavior with water play toys and inflatables
- First aid for choking
- First aid for bleeding
- Appropriate behavior on the deck and in the water

VARIATIONS   By teaching individuals in different age groups, lifeguards can gain a great deal of insight into patron behavior. The more groups a lifeguard teaches, the more knowledgeable he will become. Your teaching lifeguard is your ambassador for safety in your program.

WHAT'S MY ZONE?

EQUIPMENT   Two to three dozen pool-safe objects that float or sink

DESCRIPTION   Lifeguards are placed at appropriate stations. Each lifeguard is instructed individually regarding her respective zone of coverage. Four additional participants—called throwers—are stationed around the perimeter of the pool. Each thrower is assigned a number and is given six to eight pool-safe objects. When the leader calls out a number, the thrower whose number is called throws an object into the water. As soon as the object hits the surface, the lifeguard who is responsible for the zone in which the object lands calls out "Mine."

The leader continues to randomly call numbers until all objects have been thrown. Lifeguards continue to call out "Mine" if an object lands in their zone. Having lifeguards establish a clear idea of where zones start and stop is critical to victim recognition and timely response. If no guard calls out "Mine" for an object, this means no one is covering that area of water. If two guards call out "Mine" and the object has been thrown into an area where zones clearly overlap, all is well. If two guards call out for an object that is NOT within a zone overlap area, confusion exists regarding coverage.

VARIATIONS

- This activity may be scored. Each guard who correctly responds is given a point for the correct call. A point is deducted for each incorrect response, lack of call, or confused call.
- Change the zone configuration in the same manner it might be changed based on bather load in the facility.

ZONE ART

EQUIPMENT   One set of pool outlines and pencils

DESCRIPTION   Create a set of pool outlines. A single pool outline is just that—a line drawing of the outline of a swimming pool (see illustration).

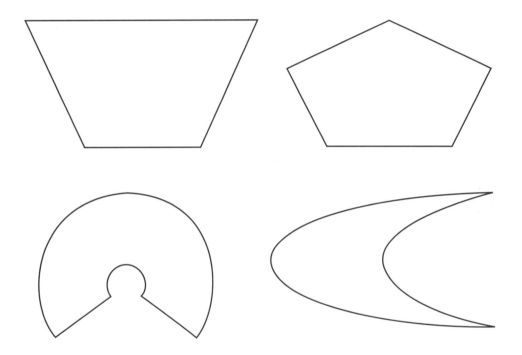

Each pool outline should be on its own piece of paper (make copies for participant use, but keep a master set). Each participant is given a different pool outline, and participants are asked to position lifeguards and establish zones for each guard position. If necessary, provide more specific directions by asking participants to mark guard positions with an X and to shade the zones using a different direction line for each guard's zone. Completed outlines should look like the following illustration.

When all participants have completed the zone coverage shading, participants should exchange papers and then evaluate the zone design of the paper they receive. When evaluating zone placements, each participant should keep in mind the following questions:

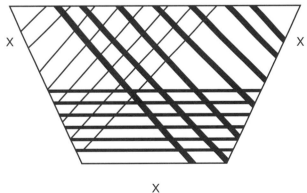

...continued

- Are all areas of the pool covered by a lifeguard?
- Is the positioning of the lifeguards appropriate to the design of the pool?
- Is the placement of the zones conducive to appropriately timed scanning patterns?

VARIATIONS   This task may be made more difficult by asking participants to add additional facility markings to the original outline drawings. Here are some of the items that might be added:

- Depth markings
- Ladders
- Diving boards
- Specific attractions, such as slides and sprays
- Lane or lifelines
- View obstructions such as trees and shade umbrellas

Aquatic Rescue
Skill Activities

4

To efficiently learn any rescue skill, lifeguards need to move through an appropriate skill progression. The learning process usually begins with information being presented in text, audiovisual, or lecture formats, and it progresses to talk-throughs and walk-throughs on land. This is quickly followed by practice in shallow water and then in deep water, using simulations that involve unresponsive and then responsive victims. For learning rescue skills with multiple parts, the best method is often to start with the performance of one single part, and then add subsequent individual parts until all parts are included. Games and activities can be used at any stage of any progression.

Introducing a skill through a game can be just as productive as using an activity to practice the application of skill combinations. When lifeguards need repetition to learn a skill, a game or activity can break the monotony that usually accompanies repetition. Applying skills in a variety of situations in games and activities will help students learn to apply any necessary skill in any rescue situation.

Although games and activities can be fun, you must remember that their primary purpose is skill reinforcement. Therefore, you should always do the following:

- Provide feedback and correction on the participants' performance of the skills. At first, you should provide just the most important feedback. With successive performances, add comments and change the participants' focus as needed.

- Begin by conducting the activities in calm water or pool water. Move to rough or open water as participants' skills and conditioning are improved.

- Be sure to explain the theory behind the practical applications, giving concrete reasons for the use of specific skills and the standards of skill performance. Winning or succeeding at the game or activity should not overshadow skill performance as the most important factor.

Rescue skills may be learned individually, but those skills must be implemented in combinations for any rescue attempt to be successful. Any activity or game requiring skill combinations also reinforces the types of thinking and actions necessary for emergency responses. The greater the number of skills required for response in the activity, the more like a real rescue the activity becomes.

Rescue simulations also require a victim. A rescue manikin is a good place to start. Implementing victim practice with a manikin has several advantages. First, a manikin allows a lifeguard to practice alone and thus work on personal skills. A manikin is also able to stay on the pool bottom for an unlimited amount of time, unlike a human victim who must surface for air (often just as the rescuer is implementing the rescue). A rescue manikin is difficult to damage; therefore, using a manikin enables lifeguards to make errors until techniques can be perfected. Manikins do not bruise. Lastly, a manikin can be hidden and remain undiscovered until the rescue attempt is in progress. This is important for practice of open-water searches.

Several types of manikins are available on the commercial market. Full-body, submersible CPR manikins are the most expensive option. Manikins that include the head and trunk only are less costly; these manikins are made of heavy-duty plastic and are weighted to simulate normal body weight. A homemade water manikin can be put together using a regular clothing manikin (plastic). The clothing manikin needs to be weighted and dressed. (To find suppliers of rescue manikins, consult the list of product suppliers in the appendix.)

When a person is playing the role of the victim in a rescue simulation, every effort must be made to ensure that the simulation is realistic. For victims on the surface of the water, this is fairly easy. Even in a facedown position, a victim can sneak a quick breath as needed while continuing to maintain the appropriate victim posture. For victims on the bottom, this becomes much more difficult. The average swimmer cannot stay prone on the bottom of the pool or lake, waiting for a rescuer to arrive. Many individuals have difficulty even submerging to a lying position (prone or on their side), much less remaining motionless. However, a swimmer with good breath control can usually be a good underwater victim by wearing a weight belt.

Scuba belts come with a variety of weights that can be placed on the belt and adjusted as needed. Eight pounds (3.6 kg) of weights is usually sufficient to assist most lifeguards in reclining on the bottom long enough to be a realistic victim.

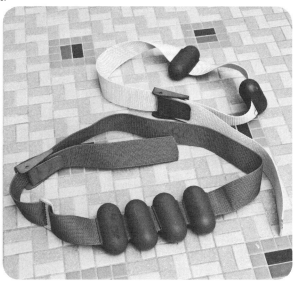

Scuba belts have quick releases, allowing a victim to release the belt before being placed on a backboard or lifted to the deck. Combining the use of a weight belt with a well-timed victim submersion allows a rescuer to have a more realistic rescue attempt.

Don't forget open water. Lifeguard training often takes place in a pool setting, and many of the activities and games in this chapter are designed for use in a pool. Many lifeguards train in pools but obtain jobs on lakes. The decrease in visibility is sometimes a surprise. In a pool, murky lake water conditions can be simulated by wearing a swim mask with the outside of the lens smeared with waterproof black and brown marker ink (or even Vaseline). However, training in open water is very important. Open water means a river or lake, complete with waves, wind, marine life, shoreline variances, and differences in bottom visibility. These conditions challenge lifeguards to not only swim stronger, but also apply learned techniques in new ways. All outdoor guards should be trained for a lake search and open water is preferable for practicing this skill. Many of the activities in this chapter can be used in either setting. Toward the end of the chapter, a section is provided that contains activities and games designed specifically for open-water implementation. See chapter 5 for more information on ways to practice rescue simulations.

BOTTOM TAG

EQUIPMENT   Mask, fins, and snorkel for each participant

DESCRIPTION   All participants wear masks, fins, and snorkels. A game of tag is played in deep water. Only the bottom of the pool is a safe area. Once tagged, the swimmer becomes it. Caution: Remind swimmers to surface safely by coming up with one hand raised above their heads. Appropriate clearing of mask and snorkel must occur during the activity.

VARIATIONS

- Use flag football belts, and have participants play tag by ripping the flag as a tag. If a swimmer's flag is ripped off, he must replace it by ripping the flag of another swimmer (not the person who ripped his flag). The bottom of the pool is still a safe area. Play for a specific time period; the winner is the swimmer with the most flags in his possession.

- Play the game as frozen tag. If a swimmer is tagged (or his flag is ripped), he must "freeze" on the surface until he is liberated by a tag from another swimmer (or until another swimmer gives him a replacement flag).

CLEAN THE POOL

EQUIPMENT   Dive rings, numbered dive discs, or numbered dive sticks

DESCRIPTION   Dive discs, rings, or sticks are scattered in deep water. On command, swimmers must dive and get as many items as possible in one dive. When using numbered discs, the participant with the highest point total off the discs is the winner. When using dive rings, the swimmer who brings up the most rings is the winner.

VARIATIONS

- Use many different objects (at least four or five per participant), and allow participants to perform several dives to totally clean the pool. With several dozen objects, give one point for each item without its own number (thus, not all objects have the same value).

- Divide students into teams, and score the activity on a team basis.

- Vary the point numbers. With some objects worth more than others, the search becomes more specific.

- Position the swimmers in the water, and ask them to close their eyes when the objects are scattered.

- Allow as many dives as can be done in a specific amount of time.

- Have participants perform the dives as part of a search pattern so that they can only retrieve objects while following search protocols.

CROSS BEARINGS

EQUIPMENT   One rescue tube; one blindfold

DESCRIPTION   Group participants into teams of four. Within each group, two people are on "shore." These two people are spaced apart and in good position to give cross bearings. The third group member plays the role of a submerged victim. The fourth person is the rescuer. The rescuer begins in the water at the point in the pool farthest from the victim submersion site. The rescuer puts on the blindfold. Then the victim enters the water very quietly and swims silently to the point where she will submerge. Once the victim is treading in place, the team members giving cross bearings start providing directions to the rescuer, who then begins to swim to the bearing cross point. When the rescuer is within one body length of the victim, the victim should quickly and silently submerge to the bottom.

When the rescuer reaches the submersion site, the team members giving cross bearings should indicate that the rescuer must dive. At that point, the rescue continues as a normal submerged victim rescue. The rescuer can remove the blindfold (upward overhead) after the victim is secured on the rescue tube and before the swim to safety.

VARIATIONS   This can be a timed activity, and the rescue can be simulated by using a dropped brick rather than an actual person. Drop the brick in the same place for each team's rescue attempt. Then time each team to determine which team gives the most efficient cross bearings.

EVERYONE'S A SWIMMER

EQUIPMENT Equipment that can be used to simulate disabilities (e.g., blind-folds, triangular bandages to restrict arms or legs, splints). You need to have enough equipment so every participant can simulate each disability represented.

DESCRIPTION Lifeguards must be able to distinguish between swimmers who are swimming effectively, those who may need some assistance, and those who are actually drowning. Part of developing this ability involves recognizing that some individuals may swim differently than the expected norm. A swimmer with a disability, particularly a physical disability, may look different in the water; this swimmer might exhibit swimming skills that are unrecognizable but may still be effective and efficient for that swimmer. In this activity, lifeguards learn through firsthand experience that a disability does not mean a person is no longer capable of swimming. Rather, although a disability may change the appearance of a swimmer or how that swimmer accomplishes a task, a disability does not preclude effective swimming.

For this activity, all participants assume a disability. This might include simulating any of the following:

- Visual impairment or blindness by wearing a blindfold or goggles with smear-painted lenses
- Auditory impairment or deafness by wearing earplugs and a swim cap
- Physical impairment of hemiplegia by using a triangular bandage to tie an arm and leg (same side) to each other
- Physical impairment of amputee by tying a triangular bandage around the waist and slipping both arms into the tied bandage
- Physical impairment of rigidity by splinting an extremity
- Physical impairment of flaccid muscles by being totally limp (using no muscle strength or control)

...continued

- Cognitive impairment by impairing hearing and vision to limit informational input or by playing extremely loud music

After preparation, participants are asked to perform a variety of swimming skills. Here are some of the skills that might be included:

- Performing water entry and exit
- Leaving the pool and using the lavatory facilities
- Swimming a lap or more using a specific stroke
- Performing a surface dive and underwater swimming
- Performing safety skills and elementary rescue techniques
- Performing small craft skills

After participants perform the skills, hold a discussion with the group about how being disabled—even temporarily disabled—affected how the skill was performed. Be sure to discuss how the swimmers might have looked to a lifeguard. Ask participants, "If you were the lifeguard, would you have thought the person was drowning, rather than swimming?"

VARIATIONS

- Have participants simulate a variety of disabilities or combine disabilities. For example, someone simulating paraplegia could also be blind.
- Ask participants to extend the simulation to tasks outside the pool, such as eating a meal, shopping, getting from the parking area to the pool, and using the locker room.

Contributed by Ann Wieser, Greensboro, NC

EXTEND YOUR REACH

EQUIPMENT A variety of items that can be used for elementary rescue (e.g., a towel, kickboard, rescue tube, PFD, paddle, pole, article of clothing). You need enough equipment for each group of four to six individuals to have at least four different items.

DESCRIPTION The entire group is divided into smaller groups of four to six individuals. One person in the group is designated as the victim; this person treads water in the deep end of the pool. The rest of the group begins at the opposite end of the pool. These group members are provided with at least four different items of equipment (as previously described).

The task of the remaining group members is to perform a wading rescue. They must form a human chain and use their supply of chain-lengthening equipment to successfully rescue the victim. Each group must plan the use of its equipment. In making the chain links, once a proper chain grip has been assumed, the rescuers may not break the chain. If the chain is broken, the group must start over. On completion, the victim's hands must be placed on the deck before any link in the chain can be broken. If the chain breaks before the victim is touching the deck, the group must start over. The task is completed when the victim is rescued through the efforts of the group (using the equipment provided). Small groups may compete against each other, racing to see who can complete the rescue first, or this activity can be used to teach the value of group effort and the problem-solving process.

VARIATIONS

- If the group is large enough to have several teams, one team can perform the rescue task while the other teams create turbulence by standing along the rescue chain and making waves and splashes.
- Teams can compete to see who can make the most effective rescue—one with no breaks in the chain—or they can compete for the fastest time.

Contributed by Ann Wieser, Greensboro, NC

FOUR-MAN TUBE RELAY

EQUIPMENT   One rescue tube for each team of four participants

DESCRIPTION   Divide the group into teams of four participants each. Each team should have its own lane. The four team members are evenly distributed along the entire length of the lane. On a given signal, the first person for each team puts on the tube strap and sits on the rescue tube (straddle style). This person rides the tube, paddling with the arms and moving forward to the next person in line. When the rider reaches the next person, that person joins the first person sitting on the tube, and both paddle forward to the third person. When the two riders reach the third person, that person joins the first two participants straddling the tube.

The group of three then paddles forward to the final team member. When the group reaches that person, the person joins the other three straddling the tube, and all four team members turn around and paddle back to the start position. This activity shows participants that a rescue tube will support multiple victims. The activity also encourages teamwork while helping participants develop fitness. It can be performed as a race or simply a team-building activity.

VARIATIONS
- Have the first three participants for each team wear blindfolds. The fourth person must give verbal directions to guide the team throughout the activity.
- Vary the direction of travel during the activity.

Contributed by Ann Wieser, Greensboro, NC

GEAR RETRIEVE

EQUIPMENT   One set of mask, fins, and snorkel for each participant

DESCRIPTION   Before this activity, participants should be comfortable with fitting, wearing, and clearing a mask and snorkel. They should also be comfortable wearing fins. Each participant tests her equipment for fit. Then, each participant drops her mask, fins, and snorkel into the water (the water should be 7 to 9 feet [2.1 to 2.7 m] deep). After the equipment has sunk to the bottom, each participant enters the water with an ease-in entry (so there is no diving advantage from a headfirst entry), swims to a point above her gear, uses a feet-first surface dive, and retrieves her gear. Once participants begin the surface dive to pick up their gear, they may not lift their face out of the water until all gear has been put on and cleared. It is not necessary to pick up all gear on the first dive. Although participants can put on the gear in any order, the best strategy may be to put on and clear the snorkel first, and then put on and clear the mask and fins. Working with the snorkel first will be an advantage because, once the snorkel is cleared, it may be used for breathing. Caution: Do not allow a participant to hyperventilate before making the gear dive. Hyperventilating can cause a swimmer to lose consciousness during underwater swimming.

VARIATIONS
- Add a task, such as swimming a pool length, that participants must complete after all gear has been put on.
- Position the participants at one end of the pool, and drop the gear at the opposite end. This forces the participants to swim a length before diving for the gear.

LEAPFROG

EQUIPMENT   None

DESCRIPTION   Participants are divided into two teams. Each team lines up single file in the water, perpendicular to the deep end of the pool; teams should be lined up with at least a lane width between parallel team lines and away from the sides of the pool. The object for each team is to reach the opposite end of the pool (or another predetermined point) by leapfrogging over each other. To begin, the last person in line places his hands on the shoulders of the person directly in front of him and says, "Ready." He then immediately submerges that person by pushing down on the person's shoulders, and goes over that person straddle (leapfrog) style.

When a person feels someone's hands on his shoulders and hears "ready," the person should immediately take a bite of air, duck his chin, and submerge (just as he would if being grabbed by a victim). After going over one person, the last person in line continues going over the people in line until advancing all the way to the front of the line. As soon as a person is in the last position, he begins leapfrogging the entire line ahead. The first line to reach the other end of the pool wins. Caution participants not to kick while leaping—someone could get kicked in the head. This game is best played in deep water. If the game is played in shallow water, you should warn participants not to push down too hard (the person going under can hit the bottom and sustain a spinal injury). Instruct participants that they should leap when their arms have straightened during the downward push. Leaping when the elbows are bent could result in hitting or landing on the neck or head of the person the leaper is going over.

VARIATIONS   Omit the "ready" warning. Submerging swimmers should go under when they feel the touch of the person behind.

MANIKIN RESCUE

EQUIPMENT   Submersible rescue manikin; a variety of rescue equipment

DESCRIPTION   It is not always easy or appropriate to have a human playing the role of the victim during lifeguard training. Submerged victim rescues are particularly difficult because humans cannot always stay on the bottom long enough for novice rescuers to perform a correct rescue. During those beginning practice sessions, a submersible manikin can be very helpful.

Rescue manikins can be used for a variety of skill drills, including the following:

- Surface dive and retrieve
- Swim, surface dive, and retrieve
- Swim, surface dive, retrieve, and carry back
- Spinal injury retrieve
- Spinal injury retrieve and carry back
- Spinal injury rescue and backboard placement
- Spinal injury rescue, backboard, and strap down
- Timed swim with victim carry
- Other drills involving the use of a diving brick
- Transition from water rescue to deck resuscitation

Submersible manikins are available commercially in full-body and torso-only sizes. You can also design a submersible manikin from a store clothing manikin made of plastic or fiberglass. Add weight to the hollow interior of the manikin. Then, just add a swimsuit or other clothing.

VARIATIONS

- Dress the manikin. Clothing will change the surface texture, making the manikin more difficult to grasp.
- Vary the setting for the manikin drills. In open water, it may be impossible to find a manikin without hand searching the lake or river bottom. If using a manikin in open water, be sure to use cross bearings to establish the manikin drop location. Monitor the current for possible shifts in the manikin's location once submerged.
- Vary the victim size and weight by using child manikins as well as adult manikins.
- Using manikins of different skin color, particularly during open-water training, can challenge the lifeguards' victim recognition skills.
- Blindfold the rescuer for an additional challenge.

MURKY WATER

EQUIPMENT   Face masks with the lens smeared with waterproof paint or Vaseline (one mask for each rescuer in the search line); search equipment for each person in the search line; rescue tubes

DESCRIPTION   This activity is set up in a pool as practice of an underwater search pattern. However, search participants wear the masks with occluded lenses, giving them a sense of searching in a murky lake or river. Caution: Do not use goggles for this activity. Goggles should not be worn during deep-water submersion activities because the increased pressure can cause eye damage or blindness.

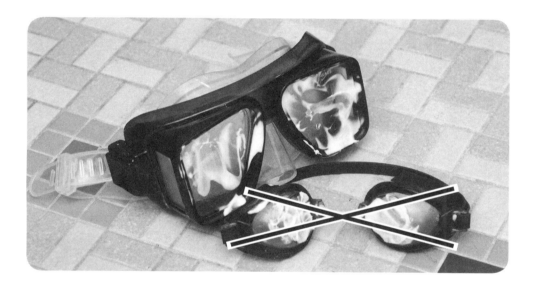

VARIATIONS

- Vary the amount of vision allowed through the mask. Have some masks with minimal occlusion and others with very dense occlusion.
- Vary the number of participants on the rescue line. Some searches will end quickly; others will be prolonged because only a few individuals are searching a large area.

PICK-UP

EQUIPMENT   A dozen dive rings

DESCRIPTION   Swimmers are divided into two teams. The two teams line up in the water, on opposite sides of the deep end of the pool. One dive ring is tossed into the water midway between the two teams. On a predetermined signal, the first person in each line races to retrieve the object. The person who retrieves the ring first then returns it to her respective team line, placing it on the deck. The team with the most successful retrievals wins. (During this activity, the leader must periodically collect dive rings as the activity continues.)

VARIATIONS

- Number off each team, and call one number from each team for the race to the object. You may call the same number or different numbers for each side. Varying the numbers will result in different competitive pairings. When using several numbers, delay the call until the ring is on the bottom.

- You could also drop more than one object and call members from each side equal to the number of objects dropped.

- Substitute a brick or rescue manikin for the dive ring. The person who retrieves the brick or manikin can then just drop it again.

RESCUE A SWIMMER WITH A DISABILITY

EQUIPMENT   Equipment that can be used to simulate disabilities (e.g., blindfolds, triangular bandages to restrict arms or legs, splints); rescue tubes

DESCRIPTION   Participants may be grouped in partners, or one person may be designated as a victim for several rescuers. The victim assumes a disability. This might include simulating any of the following:

- Visual impairment or blindness by wearing a blindfold or goggles with smear-painted lenses
- Auditory impairment or deafness by wearing earplugs and a swim cap
- Physical impairment of hemiplegia by using a triangular bandage to tie an arm and leg (same side) to each other
- Physical impairment of amputee by tying a triangular bandage around the waist and slipping both arms into the tied bandage
- Physical impairment of rigidity by splinting an extremity
- Physical impairment of flaccid muscles by being totally limp (using no muscle strength or control)
- Cognitive impairment by impairing hearing and vision to limit informational input or by playing extremely loud music

The victim with a disability then assumes the role of a drowning victim and must be rescued according to appropriate lifeguard techniques. This rescue should include removal from the water or assistance to safety. After the rescue, discuss with participants what modifications they had to make to their rescue technique in order to accommodate for the disability.

VARIATIONS   If one person is assuming the victim role for several rescuers in succession, have the victim change the type of drowning simulated from rescuer to rescuer. Do not tell rescuers what type of rescue should be performed. Be sure everyone has a chance to be a victim as well as a rescuer.

Contributed by Ann Wieser, Greensboro, NC

RESCUE BOARD MAZE

EQUIPMENT   A variety of buoyant objects (such as kickboards, PFDs, water toys, and exercise noodles); hula hoops, plastic jugs, or rescue tubes with weight tethers; rescue boards

DESCRIPTION   The buoyant objects are scattered around in the area to be used for rescue board practice. The hula hoops, plastic jugs, or rescue tubes are also distributed throughout the practice area; they are tethered vertically. Instruct participants that they should view the scattered equipment as if it were either swimmers enjoying a recreational swim, aquatic debris (weeds, leaves, tree branches, and other open-water litter), or both. Rescue board practice is then held in this environment.

Participants can paddle through the maze for accuracy, trying not to bump anything. They can also paddle a specific path through the maze in a race against time. Lastly, a victim can simulate distress or drowning, and the rescuer must complete the appropriate rescue board rescue without being deterred by the objects in the water. This will be particularly complicated if the rescue involves a submerged victim, because a variety of rescue skills will come into play to accomplish the task.

VARIATIONS   Vary the activity by changing the type of rescue to be performed, as well as the arrangement of the scattered equipment.

Contributed by Sue Skaros, Milwaukee, WI

RESCUE BOARD PULL-UPS

EQUIPMENT   Rescue boards

DESCRIPTION   Starting in deep water, each participant attempts to mount his rescue board from the side (rather than from the end). The person must pull himself up onto the board without causing the board to tip over (similar to getting into a swamped canoe).

VARIATIONS   Vary the side location for mounting. Mounting from the center of the long side will be very different from mounting from a forward position or one toward the back corner of the board.

Contributed by Sue Skaros, Milwaukee, WI

RESCUE MAZE

EQUIPMENT   A variety of buoyant objects (such as kickboards, PFDs, water toys, and exercise noodles); hula hoops with weight tethers; rescue tubes

DESCRIPTION   The buoyant objects are scattered around in the area to be used for rescue practice. The hula hoops are also distributed throughout the practice area; they are tethered vertically. One rescue tube is reserved for the participant who is the rescuer. The other rescue tubes are also scattered in the rescue area. Instruct the participants that they should view the scattered equipment as if it were swimmers enjoying a recreational swim or as aqua debris (weeds, leaves, tree branches, and other open-water litter). Rescue practice is then held in this environment.

The victim simulates distress or drowning, and the rescuer must complete the appropriate rescue without being deterred by the objects in the water. This will be particularly complicated if the rescue involves a submerged victim because the rescuer's tube could possibly become tangled in the "weeds."

VARIATIONS   Vary the activity by changing the type of rescue to be performed, as well as the arrangement of the scattered equipment.

RESCUE TUBE CHALLENGE

EQUIPMENT   One rescue tube for every two participants

DESCRIPTION   Participants work in pairs. One person dons the rescue tube and must swim while pulling the other person (as in a tired swimmer assist) for one length of the pool. Then they switch. The role of the second person is to offer as much resistance as possible without touching the bottom. With a pool full of people, this can even create waves! The activity can be performed as a race or just for fun.

VARIATIONS

- Add tethered floating obstacles so that lifeguards must tow victims through an obstacle course.
- Have both participants wear sweatpants and sweatshirts for added weight and resistance.
- Have one lifeguard tow two swimmers on the tube. See how many swimmers a single rescuer can tow.
- Specify the kick to be used when towing.

Contributed by Sue Skaros, Milwaukee, WI

RESCUE TUBE TUG-OF-WAR

EQUIPMENT   One rescue tube for each person

DESCRIPTION   Divide the group up into pairs; each person should have a rescue tube. Each person dons his tube and extends the opposite end to his partner. Each swimmer ends up holding two tubes—his own tube and the nonstrap end of his partner's tube. Starting from the middle of the pool, each person tries to kick back to his own side of the pool, pulling his partner with him. Letting go of the other person's rescue tube disqualifies a participant.

VARIATIONS

- Try this activity with participants pulling toward the ends, rather than the sides, of the pool (again starting at the center of the pool).
- Specify the kick to be used for towing. No touching the bottom!

Contributed by Sue Skaros, Milwaukee, WI

SCAVENGER HUNT

EQUIPMENT   Masks, fins, snorkels, old towels, bricks, and a variety of objects

DESCRIPTION   Assemble a variety of sinkable objects, such as caps, cap straps, numbered diving discs, diving rings, broken padlocks, washcloths, and other small clothing items. Be sure nothing is small enough to go through the main drains. Using these items, make lists for a scavenger hunt. Write the lists on old towels. Use permanent Magic Marker to write on the towels; write big.

Make sure the list includes an item for which there is only one of that item in the pool. This item will distinguish the winner. Use a brick to anchor each towel on the bottom. Scatter all hunt items into the pool. Wearing masks, fins, and snorkels, the participants read the list while underwater. Participants then hunt the pool for the items on the list. The first team to find all the items on its list wins.

VARIATIONS

- Have participants perform the activity without the mask, fins, and snorkel. However, caution participants not to wear goggles when searching for items in deep water (this could cause permanent eye damage).
- Allow participants to hunt for only a specific period of time.

SHARK'S TEETH

EQUIPMENT   Two dozen wine bottle corks

DESCRIPTION   Swimmers are divided into two teams of at least four players each. Teams line up on one side of the pool. The corks are thrown into the water (in the middle of the pool). On a signal, all players use a stride jump to enter the water. Each player attempts to recover a cork by getting it between her teeth. Players cannot touch the cork with their hands. Swimmers then carry their cork back to the deck, climb out, and drop the cork into a bucket. The first team to have all swimmers back on deck gets one point for each cork. After a quick wash of corks in a sanitizing chlorine bath (one-fourth cup of bleach per gallon of water), toss them back into the pool and repeat the drill.

VARIATIONS

- Have participants perform Shark's Teeth using a rescue tube.
- Add to the distance that participants must swim to reach the spot where the corks are dumped.

SINKER

EQUIPMENT   Scuba weight belt and several 2-pound (0.9 kg) slide-on weights

DESCRIPTION   Place four to six slide-on weights (two pounds each) onto the belt. The person designated as the victim for submerged victim rescue then puts on this belt. The belt should be placed just above the pelvic bones. The additional weight will help the practice victim stay submerged. It will also provide additional drag to challenge the strength of the rescuer.

When the rescuer and victim reach safety, the victim can easily reach to her waist and release the belt before she is removed from the water by the rescuer. Caution: The victim should not leave the belt on during a lift out of the water. If the victim is placed down onto the weights, this could cause discomfort and injury.

VARIATIONS   Include the use of the weight belt during rescues of victims on the surface. This will add weight and drag during the rescue effort.

SPEED SHUTTLE

EQUIPMENT   None

DESCRIPTION   Swimmers line up on deck along the deep-end side of the pool, facing the opposite deep-end side (they do not swim toward the shallow end). On a two-count start, swimmers perform a stride jump into the water, do an approach stroke to the opposite side, climb out of the pool, and assume a ready position for another stride jump. While swimmers swim, the leader (starter) counts five counts very loudly. Swimmers must complete the swim and be ready to jump again in five seconds (time may be adjusted for larger pools). After the five-second count, the leader again gives a two-count start, and swimmers jump in and return to their starting point, again swimming, climbing out, and assuming a ready position in five seconds.

This cycle is then repeated. Each time a swimmer makes it across in five seconds and is ready to jump, the swimmer receives one point. If a swimmer is not ready to jump, no point is given, and the swimmer must wait on deck at the side where he is located until the line of swimmers returns to that side of the pool. Then, the swimmer reenters the game. Swimmers should not be jumping from both sides of the pool at the same time. Note: As swimmers tire, they will miss a round or two. That's all right. They should get back into the game as soon as the line comes to their side of the pool. It's the total points that count.

VARIATIONS

- Specify the particular stroke to be used.
- Add an additional skill or stunt to the swim pattern—for example, jump, swim to the second line, do a feetfirst surface dive and touch bottom, surface, continue the swim, climb out. Of course, if an additional challenge is added, the counted time must be adjusted.
- Have participants perform Speed Shuttle with rescue tubes.

SURVIVING THE CHALLENGE

This activity is divided into three segments. Each segment could be performed as an individual activity. However, the objective is for participation to be progressive, with swimmers moving from one challenge to the next. Swimmers begin with scanning, progress through a weight-carrying swim, and finish with a breathing activity. You can have all participants advance from one activity to the next, or you can only allow a specific number of "survivors" (highest scoring participants) to advance to the next activity. Because this is a multiple-part activity, all equipment should be readied and at poolside before the start of the first challenge. If the challenge is to run continuously, all equipment should be in place—either in water or on deck—before the start of the first event. This will increase the total difficulty.

SCANNING

EQUIPMENT   Four or five clear plastic bottles of various sizes for each participant. Be sure the bottles are clean and free of paper labels.

DESCRIPTION   Fill the bottles to varying levels with water. The object is for some bottles to float and for others to sink to varying depths. Station participants on deck; they should be positioned at imagined guard stations around the pool. Ask the guards to close their eyes. Then scatter the bottles throughout the water area. On a predetermined signal, the guards open their eyes, enter the water appropriately, and begin retrieving bottles. As each bottle is retrieved, the guard must return it to his guard station (the place where he began) before he can retrieve the next bottle. The winner—or survivor—is the guard who retrieves the greatest number of bottles.

VARIATIONS

- You can conduct this challenge as a timed event, rather than run the challenge until all bottles are retrieved. The survivor is the person who retrieves the most bottles in a specific time.

- Guards can work in pairs. One partner is on the deck, spotting the bottles and directing the rescuer in the water.

- Different size bottles can have different point values. Smaller bottles should have greater point value because they will be more difficult to find.

CARRY YOUR WEIGHT

EQUIPMENT   Several types of weighted objects (these may be 10-pound [4.5 kg] bricks, plastic bottles full of water, sweat suits, rescue manikins, or any other heavy object that is pool safe); a bathroom scale

DESCRIPTION   All heavy objects are placed in a central location in deep water. Station participants on deck; they should be positioned at imagined guard stations around the pool. On a predetermined signal, the guards enter the water appropriately and begin retrieving weighted objects. Each retrieved item must be returned to the guard's station before the guard can retrieve the next item. The survivor is the guard who has retrieved the most weight at the completion of the challenge.

VARIATIONS

- You can conduct this challenge as a timed event, rather than run the challenge until all objects are retrieved. The survivor is the person who retrieves the most weight in a specific time.
- Guards can work in pairs. One partner is on the deck, spotting the objects and directing the rescuer in the water.
- Objects of different weight can have different point values. Heavier items should have greater point value because they will be more difficult to retrieve.

YOU LEAVE ME BREATHLESS

EQUIPMENT Metal boxes; two balloons for each box; one pair of gloves for each box; shade cord or lightweight rope

DESCRIPTION Place two balloons into each metal box; these boxes represent first aid kits. Close the box and then tie the cord or rope all around the box. Make lots of knots! Each box should have about the same amount of roping and knotting. Place the boxes on deck at one end of the pool.

Assemble the guards in a line along the other end of the pool. On a given signal, the guards enter the water appropriately, swim to the opposite end of the pool, and exit the water. As soon as a guard is on deck, he takes a box (first aid kit), unfastens the tie-downs, puts on the gloves, and blows up the two balloons to a specified size. The survivor is the guard who is first to inflate his two balloons.

VARIATIONS

- Increase the distance that guards must swim to obtain the boxes.
- Increase the number or size of the balloons in the boxes.
- Specify the stroke to be used for the swim.
- Have participants perform the swim on rescue tubes.

Contributed by Tia Fizzano, Wallingford, PA

SWIM AND REVERSE

EQUIPMENT   None

DESCRIPTION   Swimmers line up along the pool wall at one end of the pool. Count off swimmers so there is only one swimmer per lane swimming at one time (1s, 2s, 3s, 4s, 5s, 6s). On the call of "1s SWIM," the 1s start swimming a designated stroke toward the opposite end. After allowing about six strokes, the leader blows a whistle, signaling swimmers to reverse and hold position (just as they would when approaching a victim). Check to see that swimmers are horizontal with their feet toward the direction of travel (their imaginary victim). Then, signal "1s and 2s SWIM." Allow both wave lines to swim about six strokes and again whistle for a reverse. Continue alternating swim and reverse, adding wave lines each time.

Keep the pattern moving until all swimmers reach the opposite end of the pool. Repeat the drill, moving the group in the opposite direction.

VARIATIONS   Have participants use equipment, either swimming on a rescue tube or dragging the tube and pulling it in with each reverse (releasing it again with each swim). This activity can also be performed in conjunction with the Clothes Swim (see page 33).

TIPPY BOARD

EQUIPMENT   Rescue board; four or six empty plastic milk jugs or bleach bottles; two or three 8-foot (2.4 m) lengths of rope

DESCRIPTION   Each empty jug is filled with water and tied to an end of one of the lengths of rope. Each eight-foot length of rope should have a jug tied onto both ends of the rope. Then the ropes are placed across the rescue board so that one jug for each rope hangs off either side of the board.

The jugs do not have to hang an equal distance off both sides. Rather, having the jugs hang off unevenly will enhance the experience. Place the ropes midway or farther toward the back end of the board, but not so far back that they fall off. Then the rescuer mounts the board in the usual fashion and paddles the board to a designated point and back. The hanging jugs will not only add to the weight, but will also unbalance the board. In addition, the jugs will add drag to the board, making it more difficult to paddle (thus simulating open-water conditions).

VARIATIONS   The more jugs added, the greater the physical challenge will be. This activity can also be combined with Rescue Board Maze (see page 107).

Open-Water Activities and Games

Many of the activities in this book can be used in open water. In some activities where equipment is placed on the bottom, such as Manikin Rescue (see page 103), cross bearings should be used to place the equipment. This helps ensure that the equipment can be found again if the participants do not succeed in their task. Note: For any open-water activity involving small craft, all laws and regulations regarding use of personal flotation devices should be observed. The following activities are specifically designed for open-water implementation.

BLIND SLALOM

EQUIPMENT   One rescue board or canoe and paddles; an anchored buoy; a blindfold

DESCRIPTION   The buoy is anchored 40 to 50 yards (37 to 46 m) out from shore. This activity requires participants to work in partners. One of the partners is designated as the paddler; this person puts on a blindfold. The other partner is designated as the passenger and takes a place on the board or in the canoe. The passenger then provides directions to the paddler to navigate out to the buoy and back to shore.

VARIATIONS
- Add an additional blindfolded paddler. The two paddlers are required to work as a team, under the direction of the passenger.
- Use a duplicate set of equipment and conduct this activity as a race. This activity can also be a relay; the same passenger provides directions to a team of paddlers, and each individual makes one trip out and back.

CANOE YOUR BOARD

EQUIPMENT   One rescue board, one canoe paddle, and one buoy and anchor

DESCRIPTION   The buoy is anchored 40 to 50 yards (37 to 46 meters) from shore. The participant is provided with a canoe paddle and a rescue board. The participant's task is to use the canoe paddle—and only the canoe paddle—to propel the rescue board out to the buoy and back to shore.

VARIATIONS

- Specify the paddling position (sitting, kneeling, or standing on the board).
- Use a duplicate set of equipment and conduct this activity as a race between two participants.
- Have teams of two perform this activity; each participant has a canoe paddle. Teams of participants can also perform this activity as a relay; each participant performs one trip out and back.
- Vary the course. Instead of an out-and-back course, any type of obstacle or slalom course can be set up using buoys.

FIND THE FLAG

FIND THE FLAG

EQUIPMENT   One rescue board or rescue tube and one blindfold for every four participants; a buoy anchored 20 to 30 yards (18 to 27 m) out from shore; one colored rip flag for each group of four (each flag should be a different color). Anchor the flags to the buoy. This can be done by attaching Velcro to individual rip flags and to the buoy or by adding leash clips to the flags and D-rings to the buoy rope.

DESCRIPTION   Divide each group of four into four job classifications. One person is rescuer, one person is left cross bearings person, one person is right cross bearings person, and one person is flag return. The rescuer is blindfolded and given her rescue board or rescue tube. After the rescuer is blindfolded, the two people giving cross bearings take their positions. On a start signal, the rescuer must paddle her board (or swim while on or towing the tube) out to the buoy, retrieve her colored flag, and return to shore. Guidance, including guidance on the color of the flag, is provided verbally by the cross bearings people on the same team. These individuals not only give directional information, but also warn of hazards if the rescuer veers off course. When the rescuer returns to shore, the flag return person swims the flag out and reattaches it to the buoy as the rescuer's blindfold is removed and passed to the next person. Positions rotate from rescuer to right cross bearings to flag returner to left cross bearings. The activity is completed when each person has performed each job.

VARIATIONS   This can be a timed activity; each team tries to beat its previous time, or teams can compete with each other. If the buoy is placed farther away, cross bearings can be sighted with binoculars. The type of rescue equipment used can also be varied.

PADDLE, SWIM, PADDLE

EQUIPMENT   One rescue board; one canoe or kayak and equipment for paddling; one buoy and anchor

DESCRIPTION   The buoy is anchored 40 to 50 yards (37 to 46 meters) out from shore. In this activity, the participant makes three trips from shore to the buoy and back. On the first trip, the participant paddles the rescue board. On returning to shore, the participant leaves the rescue board on shore and then swims a repeat of the same distance. After returning from the swim, the participant takes the equipment for the canoe or kayak and paddles the craft over the same course. The participant's performance on the first day is used to establish a baseline time. Subsequent performances should result in an improved time.

VARIATIONS

- This activity can be performed as a race between two participants (a duplicate set of equipment is needed).
- Teams of three can also perform this activity as a relay; each participant performs one trip out and back. For a longer relay, each relay participant can perform all three tasks.
- Instead of an out-and-back course, any type of obstacle or slalom course can be set up using buoys.

RESCUE BOARD SLALOM

EQUIPMENT   Surface buoy markers and anchors; rescue boards

DESCRIPTION   Arrange the anchored buoy markers in a specific formation. Here are some of the typical formations used and the type of paddling required with each formation:

- Straight-line formation to require zigzag paddling
- Triangle formation to require paddling with changes in the direction of wind and waves
- Pairs of buoys separated by 3 to 4 feet (91 to 122 cm) to establish centers for figure eight paddling
- Parallel lines to require straight-line paddling
- Circle formation to require paddling with a continual pull in one direction
- Diagonally alternating pairs of buoys (set up like slalom gates) requiring frequent changes in direction

Without bumping any of the buoys, participants must paddle the rescue board around the anchored buoys in the appropriate formation.

VARIATIONS

- Time the paddlers, encouraging them to decrease their time while still maintaining clean running of the slalom course (not bumping any of the buoys).
- Have the remainder of the group at the ends doing dolphin kicks to simulate wave action.
- Combine this activity with Craft by Hand (see page 36).

Contributed by Sue Skaros, Milwaukee, WI

RING BUOY REPEATS

EQUIPMENT   One ring buoy and one anchored buoy marker for each participant; one watch with a second hand

DESCRIPTION   The buoy is anchored out from shore or dock at a distance that is three feet (91 cm) less than the length of the ring buoy's rope. The object of this activity is to make as many accurate ring buoy throws as possible in a specific length of time. On a predetermined signal, the participant makes the first buoy throw. To count as a success, the ring buoy must land past the anchored buoy and must touch the buoy as it is pulled in. Once the ring buoy lands, the participant reels in the buoy and immediately throws again, and again, and again, scoring one point for each successful throw. When the time limit has been reached, the participant stops throwing. A throw counts if the ring buoy has touched the anchored buoy. Start with three to four minutes and gradually decrease the time allowed for throws.

VARIATIONS
- Place several anchored buoys, each of a different color. As the first throw is reeled in, call a color for the next throw. Change the color called for each throw.
- Substitute a throw rope bag for the ring buoy.

TEAM SURF

TEAM SURF

EQUIPMENT One rescue board for every five or six participants; a buoy anchored 20 to 30 yards (18 to 27 meters) out from shore

DESCRIPTION This is a team activity. Participants are divided into as many teams as there are rescue boards available (five or six participants per board). Teams then gather standing in hip-deep water off shore with their boards. On a start signal, the first person on each team gets onto his board; this person paddles out and around the buoy and back to the start. When the person returns to the start, a second team member gets onto the board (behind the first person), and both paddle out and around the buoy. When the two team members return to the start, a third team member joins the first two on the board, and all three paddle the course. This continues until one team has all members on its board and has paddled the course and returned to the start. If teams are large, the board may be underwater by the time the event concludes.

VARIATIONS
- Divide teams in half, and conduct the activity as a shuttle relay. Half of the team would wait out at the buoy; these team members tread water while waiting. A person is added to the board at each end of the shuttle (shore and buoy).
- Allow noncontact interference with the other team (i.e., splashing, wave making).

TUBE SHIFT

EQUIPMENT   One rescue tube for each participant; one anchored buoy

DESCRIPTION   This activity will increase participants' familiarity with tube buoyancy in the face of wind and waves. The buoy is anchored 50 yards (46 m) out from shore. On a designated signal, participants race to the buoy, wearing their tube strap and towing their tubes. On reaching the buoy, each participant pulls in her tube and places it under her armpits. With the tube in this position, the participant swims back to the start.

VARIATIONS   Increase the number of times that participants must swim out to the buoy and back, continuing to vary the position of the tube. Add sitting straddle across the tube, sitting swing style on the tube, lying prone on the tube, and so on.

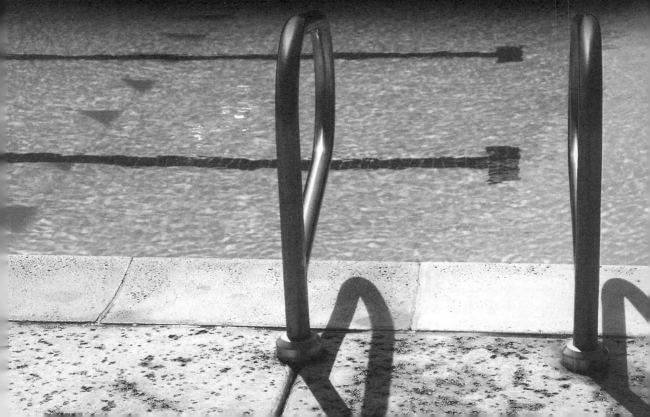

CPR, Emergency Response, and Risk Management Activities

5

Risk management activities for training lifeguards generally fall into two categories: enactment and scenario training. Enactment training is the most familiar method. It includes activities involving hands-on skill performance that enable participants to change acquired knowledge into observable behavior. Participants practice skills in order to establish habits and predictable responses based on national standards. The trainer teaches the individual skills, the students practice those skills, and then the trainer tests the students on those isolated skills. Enactment training is the heart of most national-level training programs, and it adds legal stature to the assessment of students' responses.

During enactment training, the accuracy of performance (based on skill testing) is usually clearly correct or incorrect. Enactment training helps lifeguards develop confidence in their personal skills—these skills are performed over and over again until mastery is achieved. Enactment training equips lifeguards with the skills they need to fulfill their job responsibilities during any emergency.

Scenario training is a less familiar form. During scenario training, responders must think through an entire situation, rather than just a single skill or skill sequence. Scenario training not only reinforces skills, but also educates individuals on the operation of the entire risk management plan for the facility. During scenario training, lifeguards must combine skills, make decisions, cope with unforeseen circumstances, and use judgment and discretion in their actions. See table 5.1 for further comparison of enactment training and scenario training.

Table 5.1 Enactment and Scenario Training

Enactment training	Scenario training
This training is frequently used by national certifying organizations for basic or entry-level courses.	This training is used more often in higher-level emergency response training.
Training is based on performance of single skills.	Training is based on combinations of skills.
Correct versus incorrect responses are clear.	Correct versus incorrect responses are less clear and may be judgment based.
Students are assessed by actual skill performance.	Students are assessed by discussion and scenario role playing.
Assessment determines how well individuals have mastered specific skills	Assessment determines how well individuals can implement a total response plan.
Lifeguards are assessed individually.	Lifeguards are assessed as part of the facility response team.
This training is usually the first step in the lifeguard training process.	This training usually follows enactment training, providing opportunities for lifeguards to implement learned skills, as well as combine skills into coordinated response sequences.
Lifeguards are trained in the context of their job responsibilities.	Lifeguards gain insight into the job responsibilities of everyone on the emergency response team.
Training provides lifeguards with a basic-level, universal skill set.	Training tests the application of a basic-level, universal skill set. It also provides an indication of what additional training might be needed.

Scenario training begins with developing training scenarios. A scenario is a narration of a foreseeable accident situation. Foreseeability is an important legal consideration. Lifeguards must be prepared to respond to situations that are foreseeable for their circumstance of employment. This will vary from facility to facility and from program to program.

Scenarios are more complex situations than those found in entry-level lifeguard training programs that are based on enactment training. Typical problems covered in entry-level enactment training might include the following:

- How do you open an airway?
- How would you stop two 10-year-old boys from fighting?
- How would you assist someone who said he was feeling dizzy?
- How can you stop a toddler from running on the deck?
- How can you stop a wound from bleeding?

As mentioned, scenarios are more complex and are based on foreseeability. Here are some sample scenarios:

- Open swim is in full swing when two middle-school-aged boys get into a fight in the shallow end of the pool. Several blasts of the whistle fail to end the confrontation. Rather, the situation escalates into full-scale physical engagement, with blood being drawn. Other teens gather around and start pushing and shoving, getting into the action.

- Two hours into your morning open swim, a regular participant enters your facility and reports that a man getting out of the car next to her in the parking lot has collapsed.

- A water aerobics class is in full swing. Clients are using the aqua steps at a fast pace. A participant who is late hurries in from the locker room, moving very quickly to get in and join the fun. As she nears the edge of the pool, she slips, falls, and slides over the gutter into the water. Her head enters last, hitting the deck hard as she goes in.

- It is 1:00 p.m. Women are coming in for the tot and mom swim. As the women check in at registration, your desk attendant notices that one mom seems a bit disoriented. The attendant has to repeat the locker information, and the tot is trying—without success—to get her mom to take her to the bathroom. As the woman heads off to the locker room, she staggers against the wall and stops to lean on the door jam. In the locker room, the locker room attendant notices the woman just sitting on the bench, not making any move to dress. Attempts to get a response from the woman fail.

- You are guarding at open swim when an office staff member comes into the pool to tell you that the receptionist (a normally very healthy grandmother of six) appears ill. The receptionist is having chest pains and shortness of breath.

- As the open swim group is coming into the pool, one gentleman hurries up to you, very agitated. He reports that another man in the locker room appears to be having a seizure. He further reports that the man in question is lying on the floor of the locker room, making strange movements.

- A variety of activities are going on at your facility tonight. A pool class is working in deep water. Step aerobics is in the gym. The weight room has another dozen participants. Suddenly, one of the aerobics participants comes running into the pool calling for help. Another aerobics participant was moving too quickly and fell sideward while stepping off her step; she landed hard on her right arm and shoulder and also hit her head. A large gash is bleeding profusely, and she is now unresponsive. The step instructor is a substitute who is young and new to the program.

When designing scenarios, you should vary the circumstances, situations, and projections of appropriate responses. Scenarios can be open ended, with no absolutely correct resolution. Sometimes a situation can be handled in a variety of ways, some better than others. Different lifeguards will resolve situations in different ways based on personal knowledge and skills. A lifeguard's response may also vary based on equipment available, support staff present, facility response plans, and environmental influences.

The second step in scenario training is scenario execution. This can be done in a variety of formats:

- Discussion
- Role playing
- Spontaneous discovery
- Video evaluation

Each type of format has certain advantages. When selecting a format for scenario training, consider the following factors:

- Discussion is probably the least threatening format and is a good place to start. Discussion requires no equipment, minimal space, and usually the least amount of time. Discussions can be impromptu, implemented as an end-of-class summary or used as time filler.
- Role playing requires individuals to think and move at the same time, making participation more difficult. Participants may be self-conscious in acting out roles that they are unfamiliar with. However, role playing can uncover weaknesses that discussion might mask. Finding equipment, locating people, taking time to accomplish tasks, and working with others having different job descriptions are an important part of scenario training.
- Spontaneous discovery adds elements of surprise and uncertainty, making the scenario more like real life. Caution: Be sure no actual call to EMS takes place (or that the responding EMS group is aware of the drill).
- Video evaluation provides documentation of actions. This adds the interesting aspect of comparing debriefing information with actual events, thus teaching participants about the importance of producing accurate records and reports after any emergency response.

A variety of scenario activities are included in this chapter, as well as in chapters 3 and 4. Individual and group training goals should determine the selection of scenarios and the format for scenario execution. More specific details on execution are provided with each scenario activity.

After the execution (discussion or action) of any scenario, group debriefings are used to conclude the process. During the debriefing, the group or individual who responded to the emergency should report on the response, including the actions performed and any weaknesses encountered. After this general reporting, the response is evaluated by everyone. During the evaluation, the following items should be considered first:

- How the accident or situation happened
- How the accident or situation could have been avoided
- How injury or death could have been prevented
- What rescue efforts each lifeguard would have made if he had been there
- How to correct any unsafe conditions

As the evaluation continues, more detailed questions should be considered, such as the following:

- Did planned actions accurately reflect the legal duty to respond?
- Were all actions consistent with job descriptions?
- Were all actions consistent with certification skills and knowledge?
- Were all actions consistent with how the emergency response plan of the facility is supposed to work?
- What additional training is necessary for the group, as well as for individuals?

If individuals were taking the role of their own job, each person must be sure to consider whether or not he has the skills necessary to do the tasks required by the scenario (and to do those tasks on a regular basis).

Remember, errors made during training are good things. They indicate what aspects of training need more work. How a leader handles training errors provides an example for lifeguards. As a leader, you should take a professional approach to errors. Set the standard that lifeguards must always seek to improve their emergency response by learning from their mistakes.

The activities and games in this and other chapters contain both enactment and scenario formats. Both are included to help bridge the gap between basic, entry-level lifeguard training and more advanced on-the-job training (preservice, in-service, or recertification training). These activities and games will also help participants increase their knowledge and skill level, preparing the participants to assume future leadership roles in aquatic safety and risk management.

Activities designed to reinforce knowledge and skills in CPR, emergency response, and risk management are somewhat different from those designed to reinforce swimming skills and fitness. Swimming and fitness activities provide a means to develop a skill. CPR, emergency response, and risk management activities emphasize applying knowledge or skills that have already been learned. Before engaging in the following activities and games, participants need to receive formal instruction. This instruction should adhere to the standards of a national certifying organization. In these areas, lifeguards must have the foundational knowledge and skills before applying those skills in situations of varying circumstances and difficulty.

In CPR, emergency response, and risk management activities, participants should use the appropriate personal protective equipment during any activity involving contact with a victim. Personal protective equipment may include gloves, eye goggles, body coverings, and breathing masks. Each participant should have his own personal protective equipment and should not share this equipment with other participants.

If a game or activity includes a skill—whether it is a rescue, CPR, or first aid skill—that skill should be performed in its entirety. Talking through a skill (i.e., telling how one would complete a task) is not the same as actually performing the skill. In these activities, the only task that should be simulated is the call made to 911. This call should never be actually dialed during a training activity. For the 911 call simulation, the participant can say "dialing 911," then "911 answering," and then continue by saying all of the information that is appropriate to the call.

Many of these activities are interchangeable. Taking advantage of this by varying the circumstances in the activities is very important. No two accident situations will ever be identical. A lifeguard must be able to adapt his knowledge and skills to any and every situation that arises. The more variation presented during practice, the better prepared the lifeguard will be during an emergency.

There are no winners or losers in the activities and games in this chapter. How, then, do you assess success? For each activity or game, consider the following:

- Is the participant's assessment of the circumstances correct?
- Did the participant perform critical skills correctly (skills that could determine the survival or quality of life for the victim)?
- Did the participant use equipment correctly?
- Did the participant perform critical skills without endangering himself or bystanders?
- Did the participant complete the entire activity?
- How did the participant handle extenuating circumstances?
- Did the participant maintain a professional demeanor and a mature attitude?

After an activity is complete, you should discuss the activity with the participants. Because many of these activities are simulations of rescues, this discussion can take the form of a regular debriefing. This will not only assist each participant in self-evaluation of performance, but also help familiarize the participant with the entire debriefing process. Debriefing activities are included later in this chapter.

ACCIDENT REPORTS

EQUIPMENT   Copies of the Accident Report scenarios (one per participant); copies of your facility's accident report form (one per participant); pens

DESCRIPTION   Each participant is given a copy of the Accident Report scenario, a copy of your facility accident report form, and a pen. The participant must complete the facility accident report based on the information provided in the Accident Report scenario. The scenario information is designed to mirror the thoughts that the lifeguard might have immediately after responding to the accident situation. Those thoughts must be sorted and clarified in order for the lifeguard to accurately complete the accident report. Because the accident report is a legal document, it must be completed in ink (rather than pencil), and accuracy is very important. Be sure to remind participants to report facts, not opinions. For example, in Accident Report scenario 2, the facts are that the victim experienced chest pain and shortness of breath. One opinion would be that the victim might be having a heart attack.

The samples provided here are typed; however, to be even more realistic, you could hand write the Accident Report scenario, complete with writing that is difficult to decipher. This, too, will more accurately portray the notes taken during the incident. Remind participants that they should provide a response for all items on the accident report; they should not leave any item blank. Participants may enter DNA to indicate that an item does not apply to the situation—this is acceptable because it specifies that the question has been considered, rather than ignored. Caution: The accident report form included here is intended only as a sample. It is in no way represented as a legal accident reporting form. Each facility owner or manager, in conjunction with her legal counsel, is responsible for developing an appropriate document for use at her aquatic venue or in her aquatic program. See the following examples of Accident Report scenarios and subsequent accident reports.

Accident Report Scenario 1

There was SO much blood! As I watched her finish climbing out of the pool and turn toward me, all I could see was all that blood running down her right leg. Then she looked down, saw what I saw, and started to shriek, collapsing on the deck. I pulled on my gloves as I walked toward her, and I pulled out the gauze pads from my on-body supply pouch. Those were awfully small gauze pads, and there was lots of blood. It was a good thing a bystander handed me a towel. I could hear a lady calling from across the pool, "Frannie, Frannie, I'm coming, Sweetie." Frannie's mom was really difficult to understand. She had some sort of accent. I tried to take good notes when she told me her daughter's name and information (Frannie Kopsickski, 17812 Honeymead Terrace, Plantainville, GA 63251; 818-574-9912). Frannie was such a tiny little girl, just like my little sister. I guessed right when I said she was seven years old. She just had a birthday yesterday. Pool water sure makes blood look like BLOOD. By the time I mopped up her leg, I could see a cut right in the middle over her leg bone. But, once the leg was dry, the bleeding soon stopped with a little direct pressure. When I didn't have to worry about blood anymore, I could tell her what a pretty swimsuit

...continued

she had. That brought a smile to her face, and she stopped crying. She could tell me that she had Cocoa Puffs for breakfast and had a dog named Fred. She couldn't go back into the pool with a fresh bandage on her leg, so her mom took her home. I had a lot of cleaning up to do, with all that blood on the deck, and I almost forgot to check the ladder she scraped her leg on for sharp edges. What a way to start my shift. Fifteen minutes done, and only four hours left to go. I guess even working the "nap time" 1:00 to 5:00 p.m. shift will have its moments.

Accident Report Scenario 2

Five more minutes and I would have been done for the day. Just my luck. Now it's over a half hour past my 5:00 p.m. end time, and I'm still here doing records and reports. It seemed like EMS took forever to get here. I thought for sure the man would have a full-blown heart attack right there in the middle of Li Chin's exercise class. He REALLY looked scared as we helped him up the ramp and into a chair. Good thing there were lots of towels handy to keep him from getting chilled. The exercise instructor had the man's information on her enrollment card (Franco Sanchez, 807 N. Vine, Salsbury, KY 83625; 424-387-9485). I was surprised when the man said his age was only 67. He looked as old as my grandfather, and he's over 80! The man's birthday is the same day as mine, the 9th. But mine is in September. His is a month after. We got out the oxygen, and he did feel a bit better when he took a few breaths. He was still frightened but did calm down a little when he could breathe easier. We offered to call his wife, but he said he'd wait until he was at the hospital because he didn't want to scare her. His buddy Frank Refeg would go with him to the hospital. EMS really did get here pretty fast, just five minutes after Andy Pack, our locker room attendant, made the call at 4:55. Whew, that was a close one!

VARIATIONS This activity will vary based on the accident situations used. Try to use situations that are appropriate for your program or facility. Have several participants work (individually) on the same accident situation. When each person has completed his accident report, ask participants to exchange accident report forms. Then, a second part of this activity would include a verbal or written critique of the completed report. Ask participants to look for accuracy of information, legibility, factual content, and completeness.

Accident Report 1

Date: [Extrapolate date from the date on which this activity is done.]

Last name: Kopsickski   First name: Frannie   Age: 7   DOB: [Extrapolate]

Address: 17812 Honeymead Terrace, Plantainville, GA 63251

Phone: 818-574-9912

Time of injury: 1:15 p.m.

Location: Pool, ladder in SE corner

Description of injury: 2-inch cut on front of right lower leg

Was first aid given? Yes   If yes, by whom? Lifeguard Angelica Rodriquez

If yes, what was done? Direct pressure to stop bleeding, gauze dressing, bandage

EMS called? No   If yes, by whom? DNA

EMS arrival time? DNA

Was individual taken to hospital? No   If yes, by whom? DNA

Who was notified? Mother was present.   Relationship? Mother

Witnesses: None

Name: _____

Address: _____   Phone: _____

Name: _____

Address: _____   Phone: _____

Individual completing report: Angelica Rodriquez

Signature: *Angelica Rodriquez*   Date: [Extrapolate]

Aquatic supervisor: _____   Date filed: _____

Accident Report 2

Date: [Extrapolate date from the date on which this activity is done.]

Last name: Sanchez   First name: Franco   Age: 67   DOB: [Extrapolate]

Address: 807 N. Vine, Salsbury, KY 83625

Phone: 424-387-9485

Time of injury: 4:55 p.m.

Location: Shallow end of pool

Description of injury: Chest pain, difficulty breathing

Was first aid given? Yes   If yes, by whom? Lifeguard Hu Hon

If yes, what was done? Oxygen administered by self-held mask. Victim wrapped in towels and seated in chair in most comfortable position.

EMS called? Yes   If yes, by whom? Andy Pack

EMS arrival time? 5:00 p.m.

Was individual taken to hospital? Yes   If yes, by whom? EMS

Who was notified? No one, by request of victim   Relationship? DNA

Witnesses: _____

Name: Li Chin (Ex. Inst.)

Address: 405 S. Vine   Phone: 424-865-9087

Name: Frank Refeg

Address: 765 S. Vine   Phone: 424-847-2536

    Contact information from files.

Individual completing report: Sam Ito

Signature: *Sam Ito*   Date: [Extrapolate]

Aquatic supervisor: _____   Date filed: _____

BLOODY GLOVES

EQUIPMENT   One pair of personal protection gloves for each person; a jar of ketchup

DESCRIPTION   Teach participants how to correctly remove personal protective gloves. When participants think they can perform the glove removal correctly, ask each participant to put on gloves. Then, smear ketchup all over the surface of each participant's gloves. Be sure to "bloody" the backs of the gloves as well as the palms. Then have the participants remove the gloves. Ketchup on bare skin will indicate that a participant did not remove the dirty gloves correctly.

VARIATIONS   Combine the ketchup with a substance having a noxious odor so that removing the gloves is truly an unpleasant task.

CPR BY TOUCH

EQUIPMENT A blindfold for each participant; a CPR manikin for each participant

DESCRIPTION Each participant is blindfolded. Guide each participant to her manikin. Be sure that participants and their manikins are spaced far enough apart so they do not touch each other. The activity is conducted similar to regular cued CPR practice. However, rescuers must perform all skills while blindfolded.

VARIATIONS
- Use paint-smeared goggles instead of blindfolds. This will distort vision, rather than occlude it.
- Combine this activity with Endurance CPR (see page 146), Slip 'n Slide CPR (see page 157), No Space (see page 150), or Unpredictable Challenge (see page 164).
- Have participants perform two-person CPR, including changing places, instead of solo.

DEBRIEFING

EQUIPMENT   Equipment for debriefing is discussed throughout the activity.

DESCRIPTION   Debriefing is an important part of the follow-up process for any critical aquatic incident. Completing an accurate accident report is the first step in the debriefing process. Not only is debriefing necessary for legal reasons, but it is also critical to the health and welfare of all personnel. Debriefing is an important aspect of the prevention of post-traumatic stress disorder (PTSD). During lifeguard training, potential lifeguards should become acquainted with post-traumatic stress. Then, when the unthinkable does occur, they will understand why participation in postincident debriefing is important. Scenario training provides opportunities for lifeguards to become more familiar with the debriefing process. Just as lifeguards must learn how to write facility-specific accident and critical incident reports, lifeguards should also learn the debriefing process. This process can be used in the postactivity assessment and discussion for many of the activities and games in this chapter and throughout the entire book. The debriefing process includes (but is not limited to) the following sequence of events.

First Group Debriefing

Immediately after an incident, all paper reports must be completed (see Accident Reports). Then, as soon as possible, everyone present during the incident should participate in a group debriefing. A group debriefing is confidential to the individuals participating. Each person has the opportunity—but is not forced—to tell what happened from his perspective. Guidelines for the meeting are presented to all participants at the beginning of the session. No judgments are made. Rather, this debriefing is for the purpose of sharing information about the circumstances of the incident so that everyone knows what happened. Participants are also encouraged to share their feelings, without judgmental comments from others. Although mostly informational for the group, this debriefing is also the second step in the healing process (the first step being the actual accident report). The first group debriefing can be used after any training scenario involving several participants. Each person reports to the group from his own unique perspective.

Second Group Debriefing

Within a week after the incident (or training scenario), another group debriefing should take place. Again, begin by setting guidelines related to confidentiality and nonjudgmental responses. As in the first debriefing, encourage but do not require everyone to participate. By now, most of the circumstances of the incident will be known. Focus this debriefing on feelings, reactions, and emotions—what each person is experiencing now. Continue the discussion by addressing what will happen next. If the debriefing is for a training scenario, discuss what might happen next if the scenario were real, as well as what might happen next based on the training result. Based on the circumstances of the incident, this discussion might include the following:

...continued

- How a hazardous situation has been remedied
- What training will be taking place to improve response skills
- How a staffing problem might be resolved
- Any changes in staffing schedules
- Reaffirmation of the normalcy of the feelings that individuals are having
- Discussion of the availability of individual counseling and how a person can obtain counseling services

Individual Counseling

After the second group debriefing, the aquatic manager should meet individually with each person. Individual counseling gives the person an opportunity to discuss anything she did not want to share with the group. An individual session also helps the aquatic manager determine which individuals may need additional assistance. Even during training debriefings, individual counseling may be appropriate for lifeguards having difficulty during the training process.

Any of these forms of debriefing can be used within a training format. This will not only assist participants in evaluating the activity or game, but will also acquaint the participants with the entire debriefing process and why it is so important. A variety of debriefings on special topics are included in this and other chapters of this book.

VARIATIONS   Depending on the results of a debriefing, additional steps may need to be taken to mediate the results of either a training scenario or a real-life incident. Any of the following are appropriate for additional follow-up.

Staff Training

One common factor in critical incident stress (which could lead to PTSD) is the feeling of a loss of control that is experienced by the individuals involved. Lifeguards must feel confident about their skills. Therefore, after a critical incident, staff training sessions can be used to help reestablish feelings of control during emergency situations. Skill practice is important after a critical incident. Although lifeguard training rarely involves an actual critical incident, training sessions can sometimes have unfortunate or unforeseen results. Circumstances such as an accident or an altercation among participants can generate negative and uncertain feelings, as well as serious doubts related to performance (of self or others). If this type of incident does occur, implementing staff training can help restore confidence in performance and also restore team cohesiveness.

Monitoring

One of the responsibilities of an aquatic director is to monitor staff behavior. This includes monitoring for symptoms of PTSD. Monitoring for these symptoms may be particularly difficult in situations where lifeguard employment is seasonal. PTSD symptoms can occur at any time—from a week or two after an incident to many years later. One place where symptoms may surface is during lifeguard activities and games. Activities and games will involve participation stress, but not life-and-death implications. Monitoring all lifeguards during activities may provide clues to help identify individuals in need of closer monitoring or further intervention. In general, you should watch for the following:

- Irritability.
- Reported sleep disturbances or unusual fatigue on the job.
- Recurrent intrusive thoughts regarding the same or similar incidents. These thoughts might be expressed through asking numerous "what if?" questions during activities or games. They may also be expressed by reminding everyone of similarities between the current activity and a previous actual emergency.
- Disruptive behavior or acting out.
- High arousal state, including out-of-proportion competitiveness, a high startle reflex, or an unusually quick anger response.
- Expressed insecurity about job performance.
- Avoidance behaviors, including lack of participation in activities and games, skipping training, or having excuses to sit out.
- Drop in school or job performance.
- Extreme differences from normal behavior (whatever the norm is for that individual).

If these symptoms appear or if a person involved in a critical incident requests additional assistance, it is time to refer that person to a mental health professional specializing in PTSD. PTSD can develop at any time in a person's life. PTSD can develop in anyone, regardless of age, job experience, performance confidence, general mental health, or previous critical incident experiences. Also remember that a lifeguard could have an experience outside of his work environment that might generate PTSD symptoms. You may not know the particulars of the situation, but as an aquatic manager, you should be familiar with the symptoms of PTSD. You should also be vigilant in evaluating your lifeguards' performance in activities and games, situations where symptoms may first surface. Left untreated, these symptoms can have a negative effect on a lifeguard's job performance, as well as general health and welfare. Part of lifeguard training is teaching about PTSD. Make sure your lifeguards are aware of the symptoms so that they will realize when to seek professional help. Training in critical incident management should be a three-step process. Training in accident reporting is the first step. Debriefing is the second step. The third step is knowing when to involve mental health professionals in the care and treatment of an individual experiencing PTSD symptoms (Grosse, 2001).

DISASTER DRILL

EQUIPMENT   Theater makeup (and possibly costumes)

DESCRIPTION   Many public institutions are mandated to perform annual disaster drills. Hospitals, airports, city governments, and schools often stage mock disasters for the purpose of training or assessing their staff in disaster response. Participating as victims for a drill staged at one of these institutions can be a good learning experience for your lifeguards. Why be a victim? A victim is an observer of the entire disaster drill process. A victim also gains a great deal of information about how his injury would be treated in a mass casualty emergency. Victims see professionals in action as they are triaged, transported, and cared for by medical personnel. You can volunteer your lifeguards for participation in a disaster drill by contacting hospitals or government officials in your area. Disaster drills take a great deal of planning, and they are not staged very frequently. However, once completed, they are a valuable learning experience for everyone involved.

Once selected for participation in a disaster drill, participants will be informed by the people running the drill about the types of injuries the victims should represent. The participants then assume those injuries. Theater makeup and costumes may be used to create the visual effect. Participants add the appropriate victim behavior to the situation, and the rescuers do all the rest. The physical environment for the drill is set up, the victims are put into place, and the drill proceeds. The victims stay in character until the drill personnel announce that the drill is completed. After your lifeguards are released from the drill situation, you should hold a group debriefing (refer to the Debriefing activity on page 141 for further information). Because disaster drills deal with life-and-death situations, your lifeguards need to be debriefed, making sure that what they experienced is remembered in the context of a learning situation.

VARIATIONS   Every disaster drill is different. Many factors will vary for each one, from the location of the drill to the type of local response being drilled. If a participant has already been a victim in one disaster drill, that participant should not assume the role of the same type of victim in the next drill. Variety in victim roles will provide variety in learning experiences.

DRIPPY MANI CPR

EQUIPMENT   A fully dressed CPR manikin. (If using a traditional partial-body manikin, add arms, legs, and torso. Clothe the torso and limbs, and stuff the clothing with foam to shape it like a regular person.)

DESCRIPTION   Wet down the entire body of the manikin. If the manikin is submersible, submerge it so that it becomes fully soaked. Begin the activity as if conducting regular cued CPR practice. Place the manikin victim on its belly or another position where it must be rolled during assessment. In this activity, the rescuer must perform all skills with a totally wet victim.

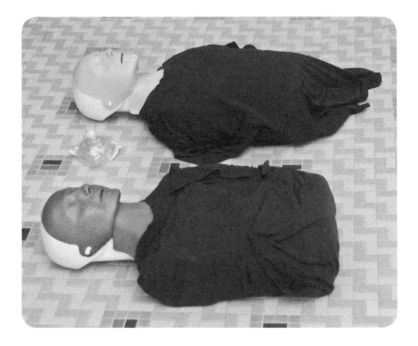

VARIATIONS
- Combine this activity with Endurance CPR (see page 146), Slip 'n Slide CPR (see page 157), No Space (see page 150), or Unpredictable Challenge (see page 164).
- Have participants perform two-person CPR, including changing places, instead of solo.
- Include adding an AED to the procedure so that the entire body and area must be dry.

ENDURANCE CPR

EQUIPMENT   One CPR manikin for each person

DESCRIPTION   Begin as if conducting regular cued CPR practice. However, maintain the practice for 10 to 15 minutes. Remind rescuers that 911 has been called. Be sure all rescuers perform all skills (instead of just talking through them).

VARIATIONS
- Combine this activity with No Space (see page 150) or Unpredictable Challenge (see page 164).
- Have participants perform two-person CPR instead of solo.

Contributed by Ann Wieser, Greensboro, NC

JEOPARDY

EQUIPMENT   This activity is based on questions and answers. Prepare a list of short-answer questions. Putting the list into a columnar format will make it easier to use (see table 5.2).

Table 5.2   Jeopardy

Answer	Question
Direct pressure	What method is the first choice for stopping bleeding?
Cardiopulmonary resuscitation	What does CPR stand for?
Red, blistered skin	What is a second-degree burn?
Armpit strap	What is the first strap applied during backboarding?
Asystole	What is the absence of heart rhythm?
Duty to act	What is the legal responsibility of certain people to provide a reasonable standard of emergency care?

DESCRIPTION   Divide the group into participating teams. You state the answer. Teams compete to see who can be first to provide the correct question. Each answer can be stated as a toss-up, where any team can answer, or teams can be addressed in rotation. If the team whose turn it is cannot supply the question within three seconds, the answer goes to the next team in the rotation, and that team has three seconds before the answer is passed again.

VARIATIONS

- Ask lifeguards to submit the answers and questions ahead of time. Tell them to focus on certification content that is difficult to remember or content that might appear on a recertification exam.

- Vary how a team may respond. When any person on a team may respond, it is possible for a strong, more competent individual to monopolize the answering experience. Rotating which team member must respond helps each team member play an equal role in the team results.

- Vary the difficulty level of the answers and questions.

- Place each answer on an individual card or piece of paper. Correspondingly, number the questions. Place the answers into a container and draw (or allow participants to draw) each answer to be used.

- Ask participants to make up the answer–question sets, and allow one team to choose and present an answer to the opposite team. This will create the effect of having participants challenge each other.

Contributed by Sue Skaros, Milwaukee, WI

MISSING TASK

EQUIPMENT   One Missing Task list for each participant; paper and pencils

DESCRIPTION   This activity enables lifeguards to review procedures (such as rescue techniques) that involve performing a sequence of tasks. Before the start of the activity, make up several Missing Task lists. A Missing Task list is a list of tasks or steps that are performed to complete a certain procedure (for the procedure to be successful, the tasks must be performed in the correct sequence). The list may be created for site-specific tasks included in the facility's emergency action plan (EAP), as well as for standardized rescue techniques. Once you have created a list, eliminate one or more items from the sequence. Rewrite the modified list, and present that list to participants, who must then decide what the missing task is (see the following examples).

Sample Missing Task List 1—First Aid for Bleeding
What is missing from this sequence?

1. Apply gauze pad.
2. Apply direct pressure.
3. Add additional gauze and continue pressure.
4. Bandage gauze in place.
5. Complete accident report.

Answer: Put on personal protective equipment (gloves) before initiating first aid.

Sample Missing Task List 2—Backboarding
What is missing from this sequence?

1. Perform ease-in entry.
2. Use spinal injury turn to place victim face up.
3. Place backboard under victim.
4. Move to stable position at side or in shallow water.
5. Apply waist or hip strap.
6. Apply ankle and leg strap.
7. Check straps.
8. Apply head blocks and secure.

Answer: Put the high chest and armpit strap on before the hip and leg straps.

VARIATIONS
- Leave more than one item out of the sequence.
- Scramble the sequence so that participants must first unscramble the sequence items and then determine what is missing.

MULTIPLE-INJURY VICTIM

EQUIPMENT   A fully dressed CPR manikin. (If using a traditional partial-body manikin, add arms, legs, and torso. Clothe the torso and limbs, and stuff the clothing with foam to shape it like a regular person.) Give the manikin victim several different injuries. Write various types of injuries on five-by-five-inch cards (and laminate the cards). Here are some injuries that could be written on the cards:

- Arterial bleeding
- Small cut
- Gushing blood
- Protruding bone
- Much swelling
- Strange joint angle
- Big bruise
- Small lump
- Strange breath odor

Place one or two cards on different parts of the manikin's body.

DESCRIPTION   Begin by having the participant rescuer survey the scene. Cue for an unresponsive victim who is not breathing. During the primary survey, the rescuer should not only encounter the breathing emergency, but also any other circumstances noted on the appropriately placed laminated cards. Some minor circumstances, such as a small cut, can be ignored for the moment. Other major circumstances, such as gushing arterial blood, will need immediate attention. In this activity, the rescuer must handle multiple problems at one time.

VARIATIONS

- Use a wet mani victim by wetting down the entire body of the manikin. If the manikin is submersible, submerge it so that it becomes fully soaked.
- Vary the number of individuals (bystanders or lifeguards) available to assist.
- Combine this activity with Unpredictable Challenge (see page 164) or No Space (see page 150).

NO SPACE

EQUIPMENT   One CPR manikin for each participant; different types of furniture (e.g., a small table, a large cafeteria table, chairs, or desks)

DESCRIPTION   This activity involves simulating a rescue of a victim who collapses in a confined space. The CPR manikin is placed in a confined location. This might be under a cafeteria table, between a chair and the wall, or surrounded by office furniture. Enact a scenario involving the participant responding to the victim in that specific confined location. Examples might include someone who

- collapses in the pool office,
- chokes while eating at a poolside picnic table,
- collapses while dressing in the locker room or lavatory, or
- falls while going out to his car.

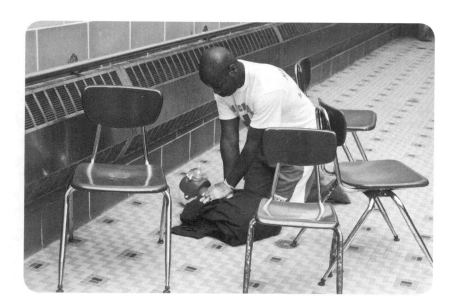

VARIATIONS
- Vary the number of bystanders available to assist so that sometimes it will be possible to move furniture out of the way and other times it will not.
- Vary the size of the manikin (adult, child, and infant).
- Vary the equipment available to the participant. For example, a lifeguard leaving work and finding someone collapsed and unresponsive in the parking lot may not have her on-body supply pouch with personal protective equipment. How would she improvise?

Contributed by Ann Wieser, Greensboro, NC

POT LUCK

EQUIPMENT   This is a station activity. The number of stations you have will determine the amount of equipment. Each station should have a CPR and AED manikin, BVM, first aid kit, bandages, splints, and personal protective equipment. In addition, each station should have a container that holds the scenario cards.

DESCRIPTION   Prepare scenario cards. A scenario card has a short description of a situation requiring an emergency response. Here are some typical scenarios that could be included on these cards:

- Victim unresponsive, not breathing.
- Victim unresponsive; air does not go in.
- Victim fell and injured right leg. No apparent bleeding.
- Victim has cut on right leg, just below knee.
- Victim has severe burn on right hand.
- Victim having trouble talking and moving right arm.

All scenario cards are placed in the container. All items of equipment are placed at each station. In addition, a station assistant is assigned to each station. In this activity, the objective is for the lifeguard to respond immediately to a previously unknown emergency situation. Lifeguards are randomly assigned to begin at any station. The lifeguard's first task is to draw a scenario card. The lifeguard reads the card out loud and then must respond immediately, providing appropriate care to either the manikin or the station assistant (as determined by the situation on the scenario card). On completion of care, the station assistant provides feedback regarding the quality of that care, and then the lifeguard moves on to a different station. The station assistant does any needed cleanup while the lifeguard rotates to the next station. The more stations available, the more quickly the rotation will be accomplished and the faster the lifeguard will have to process and apply information. Station assistants may not assist with the response. Their only tasks are to be a victim (if needed), to provide feedback based on monitoring the response, and to put the station back in order for the next participant. The station assistant also determines when the response is completed, sending the participant on to the next station.

VARIATIONS   Variation is determined, in part, by the scenarios. In addition, the amount of time spent in a response can be varied. The station assistant can end the response at any time, thus interrupting care and sending the lifeguard to a different situation. This is similar to what would occur in a triage situation. For example, a lifeguard might start out caring for someone who fell and has a suspected leg fracture; however, this lifeguard may be called away if someone else suddenly collapses and is not breathing. The more stations active at any one time, the more the lifeguard must focus on the task at hand and not be distracted by other events happening at the same time.

Contributed by Sue Skaros, Milwaukee, WI

Q & A

EQUIPMENT   This activity involves several stations. Each station should have a manikin and either a card for an emergency situation or a label for a first aid situation.

DESCRIPTION   Prepare cards for emergency situations, or prepare labels for first aid needed. Examples of emergency situations described on the cards might include the following:

- Nonbreathing victim
- Severe fall, victim unresponsive
- Fainting

Examples of labels for first aid needed might include the following:

- Severe cut (label placed on arm)
- First-degree burn (label placed on hand)
- Bone protruding from skin (label placed on lower leg)

Set up stations with manikins and labels (or cards). Divide participants into groups of two or three lifeguards per group. Groups rotate to each of the stations. At each station, each person in the group must jot down three or four critical questions she would ask to get a better history of the situation and the victim. These might be questions asked of the victim or questions asked of bystanders. The small group can discuss these questions and determine which ones are most important. After everyone has gone to each station, discuss the questions as a large group. Once the questions to be asked have been identified, discuss probable answers to the questions, bringing out as many alternatives as possible. As answers are discussed, also cover how a lifeguard would proceed with emergency treatment. This discussion should include the decision on whether the victim could be treated at the scene and then released, whether EMS would be called, or whether the victim would be advised to see her own doctor. This decision can also be discussed in smaller groups first; the smaller groups reach a consensus and then bring their decisions back to the larger group for analysis. This process can enhance participants' history-taking skills, as well as their critical decision making.

VARIATIONS   A variation of this activity can be used for practicing bandaging and splinting by having each station set up with a different type of injury. One station might only require monitoring the victim and keeping her comfortable until help arrives. Another station might involve a help-delayed situation where a splint and transportation would be appropriate.

Contributed by Sue Skaros, Milwaukee, WI

ROLE PLAY DEBRIEFING

EQUIPMENT   Equipment and apparel appropriate to each job position and the requirements of each job task; a variety of role play scenarios; role play actor cards for each person named in each scenario

DESCRIPTION   Role playing is an excellent technique for helping lifeguards develop communication and human relations skills. In role playing, each person is assigned a specific role—responding guard, assisting guard, locker room staff, pool manager, and so on. The group is also provided with a scenario of a typical aquatic incident, including what each character did during the incident. Lifeguards act out their respective roles, and then the debriefing takes place on this scenario. In role playing, individuals need to actually act out their roles, rather than just narrate what they think their character would do. Acting out the character's role allows the participant to integrate the expression of thoughts, feelings, and opinions. These are important components of human relations and the communication process.

   Divide the group into smaller groups of five or six persons each. Give each group a role play scenario and the cards appropriate for each person named in the scenario. First, the group should read the entire scenario. Then, each participant should draw a role play actor card and don the apparel appropriate to his persona. Next, the group should act out their role play scenario—not only acting out the actions described on the card, but also continuing the scenario to bring about the most desirable outcome. After the enactment of the scenario, all participants should undergo debriefing to discuss the details of this situation from everyone's perspective. In the debriefing, the group should also discuss how effectively the situation was resolved. This should include exploration of alternative ways of handling the circumstances. See the following example of a role play scenario and corresponding role play actor cards.

Sample Role Play Scenario

Seven-year-old Josiah is at the pool with his mom. They are part of about 25 people enjoying the aquatic activity on a warm, sunny day. Josiah is scooting around the perimeter of the pool, swinging on the ladders, splashing people, and hollering, "Catch me if you can," to the lifeguards. His friend is trying to keep up with him but looks as if he is afraid of the water—the friend is moving very slowly and carefully. The lifeguards need to make Josiah change his behavior, because he is not a deep-water swimmer and can only swim a few feet in shallow water. Several people have already complained about Josiah's splashing and loud behavior. How can this situation be resolved?

Role Play Actors

- Josiah: He is seven years old and spoiled. He has no behavioral limits set by his mom, and he does what he wants to do most of the time. He likes to hold onto the edge of the pool and scoot all around the pool, moving in and out of deep water at will, swinging on the ladders, splashing people, and hollering "Catch me if you can" to the guards.

...continued

- Josiah's mother: She is working on her tan at poolside. She loves Josiah and thinks that he is spirited but that he can do no wrong. She wants him to have *fun* in whatever way *he* thinks he can do that. She thinks the lifeguards pick on her son.
- Lifeguard 1: Josiah scoots right under the guard stand to swing on the ladder two feet away, splashing the lifeguard in the process.
- Lifeguard 2: This guard must cover lifeguard 1's zone if lifeguard 1 must leave the stand.
- Pool manager: This person is working in the office on paperwork.
- Friend of Josiah: He can't swim at all and is slightly fearful, but he wants to be with Josiah and play with him all the time, no matter where he is.

VARIATIONS   Role playing can be done with or without formal debriefing afterward. Any scenario can be done as a role play. Any scenario can also be used for debriefing. Combining the two activities creates the most realistic experience for participants. Maximum variety occurs when a wide range of circumstances are implemented within the various scenarios.

SCRAMBLED RESPONSE

EQUIPMENT One Scrambled Response scenario for each participant; paper and pencils

DESCRIPTION During an emergency response situation, many factors will be competing for the attention of the lifeguard, and a variety of tasks will need to be accomplished. This activity assists lifeguards in establishing priorities and appropriately sequencing their response. Each participant is given a copy of a Scrambled Response scenario. The participant's task is to unscramble the order of the items, creating a new list with the items in the order in which the tasks should be done. See the following examples of Scrambled Response scenarios.

Scrambled Response Scenario 1

EMS transports victim.

Victim's chest is dried.

Lifeguard 1 performs primary survey.

Lifeguard 1 activates EAP.

Lifeguard 1 completes accident report.

Victim experiences severe chest pain, grasps chest, and slowly sinks to the bottom.

Desk attendant meets EMS.

Lifeguard 1 checks for responsiveness.

Lifeguard 2 brings AED to victim.

Lifeguard 1 executes submerged victim rescue.

Pool manager holds debriefing.

Lifeguard 1 continues with CPR.

EMS is called.

Lifeguard 2 assists with lift from water.

Correctly reordered, this list should read as follows:

Victim experiences severe chest pain, grasps chest, and slowly sinks to the bottom.

Lifeguard 1 activates EAP.

Lifeguard 1 executes submerged victim rescue.

Lifeguard 2 assists with lift from water.

Lifeguard 1 checks for responsiveness.

EMS is called.

Lifeguard 1 performs primary survey.

Lifeguard 1 continues with CPR.

Lifeguard 2 brings AED to victim.

Victim's chest is dried.

...continued

Desk attendant meets EMS.
Lifeguard 1 completes accident report.
EMS transports victim.
Pool manager holds debriefing.

Scrambled Response Scenario 2

Victim on backboard is removed from pool.
Hip strap is applied.
Lifeguard 2 clears pool.
Victim hits head on diving board while doing dive.
Lifeguard 1 activates EAP.
Forehead strap is applied.
Lifeguard 3 brings backboard into water.
Chest strap is applied.
EMS is called.
Backboard is placed under victim.
Lifeguard 1 does ease-in entry.

Correctly reordered, this list should read as follows:

Victim hits head on diving board while doing dive.
Lifeguard 1 activates EAP.
EMS is called.
Lifeguard 1 does ease-in entry.
Lifeguard 2 clears pool.
Lifeguard 3 brings backboard into water.
Backboard is placed under victim.
Chest strap is applied.
Hip strap is applied.
Forehead strap is applied.
Victim on backboard is removed from pool.

VARIATIONS
- Lengthen the list of tasks. Include multiple victims or injuries.
- Involve differing numbers of staff members assisting the responding guard.
- Ask participants to add to the list (the sample lists do not contain all tasks appropriate to the situation). Participants should add items (in the correct order) that are appropriate to the situation, but not included in the original list.
- Perform this activity as a group task, rather than an individual one. Divide the group into several smaller groups, and provide each group with the same Scrambled Response scenario. Then, time the groups to see who can make a correct list in the shortest amount of time.

SLIP 'N SLIDE CPR

EQUIPMENT   An outdoor slip 'n slide mat, a yoga mat, or another surface covering that is slippery when wet (the surface covering should allow space for CPR performance by each participant, several participants at a time if possible); a CPR manikin for each person

DESCRIPTION   Cued CPR practice is performed as usual. However, the manikin (victim) is positioned on the slippery surface, and the rescuer must perform CPR with his base of support also on that slippery surface.

VARIATIONS

- Combine this activity with Endurance CPR (see page 146), No Space (see page 150), or Unpredictable Challenge (see page 164).
- Have participants perform two-person CPR instead of solo.
- Introduce an AED and include drying the victim and surface as part of the rescue effort.
- Alter the surface area. Use bunched-up towels under the kneeling surface to simulate uneven beach sand.

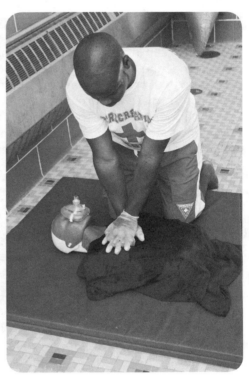

SPONTANEOUS DISCOVERY

EQUIPMENT   Equipment that is standard for the location where the training is being held

DESCRIPTION   During Spontaneous Discovery, the training day begins normally. As the day unfolds, an accident scenario is staged by a different group of people; this accident scenario is a complete surprise to the lifeguards already in training. Roles in the training group are not assigned. Rather, lifeguards function as best they can in response to the circumstances provided. Roles played by the people enacting the accident scenario (who may be students training to be lifeguards, for example) are planned ahead of time but are kept confidential to the enacting group. After the enactment and the subsequent care by the lifeguards, group debriefings are used to conclude the activity. During the debriefing, a recorder creates a record of how well the lifeguard group responded, including the actions performed well and the weaknesses encountered.

VARIATIONS   Combine this activity with Theater World (see page 161). This activity can be staged at any time and in any place. The unexpected aspect of the enactment places the lifeguard in a situation where immediate response is needed to a situation assumed, at the outset, to be real. Caution: If staging Theater World or Spontaneous Discovery during actual hours of facility operations, be sure to have an additional lifeguard present to assume the station of the lifeguard responding to the simulated emergency. This will ensure that there is no break in the surveillance of patrons at the facility.

SURPRISE

EQUIPMENT   None (other than what is available at the time of the surprise situation)

DESCRIPTION   This activity takes place during other staff training. Before the start of a training session, each person in the group is assigned a letter of the alphabet and a victim condition. Participants are asked to remember this information and to keep it a secret from the other participants. They are also instructed that if they hear their letter of the alphabet called out at any time during training, they should immediately assume the condition they have been assigned. Victim conditions might involve land situations or water situations. Here are some typical conditions that participants might be assigned:

- Fainting
- Severe stomach cramps
- Chest pain and shortness of breath
- Choking
- Severe fall
- In-water collision
- Drowning swimmer
- Drowning swimmer who grabs another swimmer
- Heat exhaustion

During the training session, at a random point in time, you call out a letter of the alphabet. Note: If the group is on land, do not call out a letter corresponding to a water situation. Do not tell participants what the letter represents. Rather, tell everyone that the closest person must respond to the situation being enacted by the individual whose letter has been called. Other participants watch and act as bystanders would. After the response is completed, discuss the quality of care given. Caution: Be sure EMS is *not* actually called during this activity. Participants should simulate any actual artificial respiration or chest compressions.

VARIATIONS
- Call more than one letter at a time, engaging several victims and rescuers.
- Sustain the activity by having participants keep their letters and conditions so the activity can be repeated during other times, such as meetings or subsequent training sessions.
- Periodically reassign conditions so that no one knows who might have which condition.
- Add specific bystander evaluation by asking some of the following questions:
    - How long did it take for the responder to not only recognize the situation but also identify the correct condition?

...continued

- Was the first response appropriate?
- Was the first aid appropriate?
- Was a secondary survey performed?
- Was the attitude of the responder appropriate to the situation?
- Have the rescuer fill out a sample accident report at the completion of the response.

THEATER WORLD

EQUIPMENT   Theatrical makeup; cold cream or other makeup remover; soap and water; washcloths and towels

DESCRIPTION   This activity can be combined with Spontaneous Discovery (see page 158) or any type of emergency scenario involving role playing. Using the theater makeup, victims in the emergency situation are made up to actually look like a victim of that emergency would look. This is particularly effective for simulating wounds and blood, as well as emergencies involving a change in skin color. It is also useful for simulations of a variety of physiological conditions in persons of color or ethnic derivation where loss of oxygenation in the blood would change skin tone. When applying the makeup, remember that this usually involves the use of a base coat. The base coat provides the foundation for the application of the makeup, and it also makes the makeup easier to remove. After the base coat is applied, the specific color and layering of texture can be done. Deeper wounds, as well as wounds with gaping skin, can also be simulated. For clues regarding the actual appearance of wounds, consult an advanced emergency response text. Most such texts have numerous color pictures that can be used as examples. Once the makeup dries, the effect is finished. Removal is done according to the directions on the makeup or with cold cream first, followed by soap and water. Caution: Be sure to ask participants about any makeup allergies before using theater makeup.

VARIATIONS   Numerous possibilities exist not only for individual victim portrayal, but also for staging multiple injuries on a single person. Using theater makeup, a staged victim could arrive on the scene and need care from a lifeguard at any time. Caution: If staging Theater World or Spontaneous Discovery during actual hours of facility operations, be sure to have an additional lifeguard present to assume the station of the lifeguard responding to the simulated emergency. This will ensure that there is no break in the surveillance of patrons at the facility.

TWO-ON-ONE PULSE CHECK

EQUIPMENT   A watch with a second hand or a stop watch

DESCRIPTION   Participants are divided into groups of three. Each person in the group is given a number—1, 2, or 3. This activity provides opportunities for lifeguards to practice counting a pulse under a variety of conditions. Initially, all three individuals are asked to jog in place. After about two minutes of jogging (which will raise individual heart rates), you call out one number as victim and the other two numbers to check pulse—for example, "2 victim, 1 and 3 pulse check." Allow a three-count start for the participants to stop jogging and to get into the positions for the pulse check. On the signal "count," the two people designated as counters begin taking the pulse of the third person. They can do a 10- or 15-second count and then multiply appropriately, or they can do a full 60-second count. The entire cuing sequence will be as follows:

"Everyone ready, jog." (The entire group jogs for two minutes.)

"2 victim, 1 and 3 pulse check." (Participants stop jogging and take positions for the pulse count; one counter is on either side of the victim, and each finds the victim's pulse.)

"Ready, set, *count*." (Counters each count the pulse.)

"Stop counting." (The counters stop. This command is given at the end of the timed count.)

Everyone participates in the initial jogging. This will place stress on the counters (rescuers) in much the same way as a full water rescue would. They will need to focus on the victim's pulse while also handling their own breathlessness. Intersperse pulse counts after activity with pulse counts after a person is lying very still for several minutes. The pulse count after activity will be easy to count. However, a pulse count during or after rest will be much more difficult to count because it will be slower and more subtle.

VARIATIONS

- Vary the exertion level and duration of the timed jog. This will also vary the elevation of the pulse.
- Combine this activity with other training activities or classroom experiences so that participants learn to count a pulse at the spur of the moment during a variety of circumstances.

UNPREDICTABLE CHALLENGE

EQUIPMENT   One CPR manikin for each participant

DESCRIPTION   This activity mixes a variety of victim conditions into one continuing rescue simulation. Starting with the rescuer surveying the scene, the situation will vary at the discretion of the leader, who indicates changes by providing ongoing verbal cues to the participants. Tables 5.3 and 5.4 provide examples.

Table 5.3   Unpredictable Challenge (Mix 1)

Rescuer's action	Leader then cues
Surveys the scene	"Scene is safe."
Checks for response	"Victim does not respond."
Opens airway and checks for breathing	"Victim is not breathing."
Gives two breaths	"Breaths do not go in."
Repeats two breaths	"Breaths go in."
Checks pulse	"Victim has pulse."
Continues rescue breathing	No cue. Allow two minutes of breathing.
Performs pulse check	"Victim has no pulse."
Initiates CPR	No cue. Allow one round of CPR. Then, provide cue at middle of cycle: "Air does not go in."
Retilts head and repeats breaths	"Air still does not go in."
Performs chest compressions and checks for foreign object	"No foreign object found" (or seen, if child or infant).
Continues chest compressions and checks for foreign object	"Gob of food found."
Sweeps out food and performs breaths	"Air goes in."
Checks pulse	"No pulse."
Performs CPR	No cue. Wait two minutes. Then, provide cue: "EMS takes over."

Table 5.4 Unpredictable Challenge (Mix 2)

Rescuer's action	Leader then cues
Surveys the scene	"Scene is not safe. Chemical spill all around."
Flushes area multiple times and distributes surface covering to make scene safe	No cue. When rescuer completes tasks, then provide cue: "Scene is safe."
Checks for responsiveness	"Victim does not respond."
Opens airway and checks for breathing	"Victim is not breathing."
Gives two breaths	"Breaths go in."
Checks pulse	"Victim has pulse."
Continues rescue breathing	No cue. Allow two minutes of breathing.
Performs pulse check	"Victim has no pulse."
Initiates CPR	No cue. Allow one round of CPR. Then, provide cue at middle of cycle: "Air does not go in."
Retilts head and repeats breaths	"Air still does not go in."
Performs chest compressions and checks for foreign object	"No foreign object found" (or seen, if child or infant).
Performs breaths	"Air goes in."
Checks pulse	"No pulse."
Performs CPR	No cue. Wait two minutes. Then, provide cue: "EMS takes over."

VARIATIONS

- Change the circumstances at will. Major points in the action where you can change the tasks include the following: during scene checks, when breaths are attempted, during pulse checks, and when any equipment arrives on the scene.
- Add the use of an AED or oxygen.
- Include a second rescuer arriving at the scene or a member of a two-person rescue team being unable to continue.
- Prolong the situation to appropriately simulate what could happen if responding professional rescuers are delayed.

UNUSUAL CIRCUMSTANCE DEBRIEFING

EQUIPMENT   One Unusual Circumstance scenario for each group of three or four participants

DESCRIPTION   Although everyone would like lifeguarding to proceed with no unusual incidents, rarely is this the case. Human behavior, an unforeseen situation during training, or even an incident reported in the community newspaper can be discussed using a group debriefing format. The incident in question is written out in detail on a card. If several versions of the incident are possible, then several versions of the incident are written. Then the cards are given to the individual groups. Each group should first read the incident. Then, the group should discuss the incident and determine what questions should be asked of individuals involved in the incident to accomplish a group debriefing. Depending on the questions asked, additional queries may be generated. When the small groups have had a chance to generate debriefing questions, each group reports to the larger group. See the following sample scenarios.

Unusual Circumstance Scenario 1—Breakup at the Pool

Mary and Juan are new lifeguard hires this season. Although they are both new to your facility, they know each other from school and have been dating for some time. Monday morning Juan arrives on time at 9:00 a.m., changes clothes, and takes his position as a deck-level guard near the diving well. The pool has been open for two hours, and because it is a hot summer day, lots of people are already in. Mary, also scheduled to come on duty at 9:00, arrives at 9:30 a.m., already wearing her suit and sporting a large bruise on the right side of her face. She looks very unhappy. Mary takes her station on the stand midway down the deck of the lap pool. At 9:45 a.m., Mary's brother Eddie arrives. He had just heard that Mary and Juan had a fight and had broken up. As he approaches Mary, he sees her bruised face. Breaking into a run, he passes Mary and heads for Juan. On reaching Juan, Eddie immediately lands a hard punch to Juan's midsection, and Juan goes flying into the diving well, almost landing on a diver who is swimming toward the side of the pool. Mary, seeing her very angry brother, and then Juan's water entry, leaves her post and runs to the well. Rico, the guard at the shallow end, sees Juan get punched and decides to help his friend. He heads for the diving well area, and on arrival, he uses a body block to send Eddie into the well on top of Juan. The sound of the melee brings the pool manager to the site. She clears and closes the diving well, and she repositions the lifeguards not directly involved in the incident so the pool is again appropriately staffed. Mary, Juan, Eddie, and Rico must undergo debriefing, and they are relieved from duty until this can take place. The other on-duty lifeguards must also be debriefed at a convenient off-duty time. What debriefing questions will you ask? Is there more than one way this situation can play out?

Debriefing questions that could be asked of each individual might include the following:

- What did you see?
- What was happening before the incident occurred?
- Did any bystanders affect the incident?
- Did you have any advance warning that this incident would occur?
- What was your role during the incident?
- How do you feel about what happened?
- What impact will this incident have on our program?
- What could we have done to prevent this incident?
- How can we prevent something like this from happening in the future?

Unusual Circumstance Scenario 2—Locker Room Photos

It was only supposed to be a short bathroom break. Merry had just relieved Keisha from guard stand 3, and Keisha was passing through the women's locker room on her way to the lavatory. As she passed the benches and lockers, she heard giggling from a group of three teens. Looking to her left, she saw a group of girls in street clothes clustered around something held in the hand of one of the girls. "She is *so* fat." (More giggles could be heard.) "And that suit!" (The girls giggled again.) "No wonder she can't pull it up. Just look at her." Keisha slowed her walk and gave the group a closer look. They were focused on a cell phone screen, and they turned their backs to Keisha as they saw her come past. Keisha altered her destination and headed for the locker room attendant at the towel desk. "What's going on?" she asked Carna. "Going on where?" replied Carna, looking up from the book she had been reading. "Over there," said Keisha. "The giggly girls with the cell phone." Just then another girl came out of the bathroom, adjusting her suit and seeming to be in a hurry. When she passed the cell phone group, they all looked up as she exclaimed, "What did you *do*?" Without pausing for breath, she then turned to Keisha and Carna and cried out, "They took *pictures*." After that cry, she lunged to grab the camera, and a full-scale physical melee broke out. Carna ran to get assistance from the pool manager while Keisha tried—without success—to break up the fight. It took the pool manager and two additional staff members to break up the fight, and the parents were as angry as the teens. Everyone had blame for someone else, and the parents of the girl whose photo was taken were planning to sue.

Debriefing questions that could be asked of each individual might include the following:

- What were you doing in the locker room?
- Where were you in the locker room?
- What did you see?
- What did you hear?
- Do you know any of these other people?
- Who else was present, where were they, and what were they doing?

...continued

- Did you have any advance warning that this incident would occur?
- How did you handle the situation—what did you say and do?
- How do you feel about what happened?
- What impact will this incident have on our program?
- What could we have done to prevent this incident?
- How can we prevent something like this from happening in the future?

Note: Some of the questions could be the same or similar for both sample scenarios. However, some questions will be specific to the individual incident.

VARIATIONS Combine this activity with Role Play Debriefing (see page 153).

VICTIMS, VICTIMS, VICTIMS

EQUIPMENT   Several manikins (some CPR, others not); first aid supplies

DESCRIPTION   This activity prepares participants to respond to situations involving more victims than there are individual rescuers to attend to them. Such a catastrophic situation might be caused by a unique weather event, an environmental accident, terrorism, or some other unforeseen circumstance of large magnitude. Set up the situation using several manikins, as well as volunteer victims, tagged with labels indicating suspected injuries. These labels might include information such as the following:

- Is not breathing, has no pulse
- Large gash in left thigh, bleeding profusely
- Slurred speech, gash in forehead
- Both hands covered with cuts
- Very anxious, crying
- Small child looking for mother
- Man with severe abdominal pain

Assign several individuals to act as bystanders. A person in a bystander role exhibits no knowledge or skill. However, a bystander can follow directions given by a lifeguard. After setting up the situation, bring the lifeguard into the scene. The lifeguard must respond using the materials available (first aid supplies and anything else available on scene). The lifeguard can also elicit help from the

...continued

bystanders. The lifeguard's response should involve providing care for the victims, rather than discussing what he would do. Bystanders should be directed to perform tasks and should be given instructions on how to complete them. Allow 10 to 15 minutes for this to occur. Then allow EMS to arrive on the scene. Additional participants can take the role of EMS personnel, and a handoff of victims can occur. Finally, end the activity and discuss the results. Here are some factors to consider in the discussion:

- Did the lifeguard triage in a timely manner?
- During triage, were life-threatening situations correctly identified and resolved?
- Were bystanders given directions?
- Were directions clear and concise?
- Were directions appropriate to the situation?
- Did the lifeguard remain calm and responsible?
- Did the interaction with EMS occur in an organized manner?

VARIATIONS

- Change the types of victims in the situation. This will change the responses needed from the lifeguard.
- Vary the setting. Staging outdoors will present a different situation from staging inside a classroom or cafeteria.
- Vary the number of responding lifeguards. Two lifeguards will need to work as a team. The more lifeguards responding, the higher the need for teamwork.

VIDEO EVALUATION

EQUIPMENT   A camera capable of making a video and audio recording

DESCRIPTION   During any type of lifeguard training that involves role playing or situation enactment by participants, a video may be made of the experience. Making a video is particularly useful for reviewing first reactions and responses, which are often the most critical factor in the overall success of the response. A video record of a training scenario is also useful for comparing what actually happened (as recorded on the video) with what the lifeguards report to have happened (each person from her own perspective). After videotaping the response scenario, ask participants to complete any appropriate paperwork, such as an accident report. Then conduct a group debriefing. Lastly, show the video and compare the video record with the paperwork reports and group debriefing. Note accuracies as well as inaccuracies. Discuss reasons for success, as well as factors that need improvement. One issue to consider is whether to inform participants that their training is being recorded. Your facility's preemployment paperwork could include a release for photo or video taking (specifying that the photos or videos are for in-facility and program use only). A video will likely be more realistic if participants are unaware that they are being taped.

VARIATIONS
- Vary the situations used for video training to closely approximate situations most likely to take place at your facility.
- Try to avoid predictability—using the same cameraperson, same video day, or same time of day—if you do not want participants to know when they will be taped.

WHAT WENT WRONG?

EQUIPMENT   One What Went Wrong? scenario for each participant; paper and pencils

DESCRIPTION   Each participant is given a What Went Wrong? scenario, along with paper and a pencil. The participant's task is to analyze the provided scenario and determine what mistakes were made during the emergency response. The participant should list all mistakes found, whether they were made by a lifeguard or a swimmer. See the following sample What Went Wrong? scenarios.

What Went Wrong? Scenario 1

It was a hot summer day, and Serena was on the shallow-water guard stand, watching the water and, if the truth be told, working on her tan in the hot summer sun. From behind her, she heard running footsteps, and a teenage boy flew past her, plunging headfirst into the pool. Watching the impact of the swimmer's head on the pool bottom at such a shallow depth (two and a half feet), Serena knew he would be hurt. Not wasting a minute, she leaped from her stand, dragging her rescue tube behind her. Landing stride in shallow water was a shock, but she was a pro, and she continued on with the rescue, blowing her whistle to move people out of the way. She found the teen facedown and not moving. Fearing he would not be able to breathe, she immediately used a hip and shoulder roll to turn him onto his back. He was breathing, and his eyes were open as he started to moan. She took this to be a good sign and tried to assist him to a stand, providing a walking support to his left side. When this failed, she called for assistance. With help from another lifeguard, Serena was able to implement a two-person lift to get the victim onto the deck and into a chair. Since the teen was still not able to speak in full sentences, EMS was called, and everyone remained on deck, waiting for EMS to arrive. It didn't take long. In just 20 minutes, Serena was back on her stand, continuing her tan. EMS had transported the teen, even taking time to backboard him. Wow, that was the first real backboarding she had ever seen. Interesting! But, just part of the job. Too bad for the teen. Rumor had it he ended up a quadriplegic.

The error list for this scenario should include the following mistakes:

- Guard stand was not shaded from hot summer sun.
- Victim was running on deck.
- Victim dove into shallow water.
- Guard used stride jump from stand into shallow water.
- Guard was dragging tube.
- Guard blew whistle late.
- EAP was not activated.
- Guard used hip and shoulder roll rather than spinal injury rescue techniques.

- Victim was not backboarded.
- Two-person lift from pool was used.
- Victim was put into chair on deck.
- EMS was called late.
- No records and reports were done.
- No debriefing was conducted.

What Went Wrong? Scenario 2

Darius was up on the deep-end guard stand, clipboard balanced on his rescue tube, completing the preopening safety checklist. It looked like it was going to be a busy morning. Over a dozen kids were already in the water, and more were coming in all the time. One kid was having a really good time climbing out, running to the diving board, taking a mighty leap off, and landing on the diagonal right in front of the ladder, ready to climb out and do it again. No swimming required. A very efficient plan. As Darius was putting the finishing touches on the report, he heard a loud scream and then lots of crying. Looking up, he saw the diving board kid down on the deck, crumpled up and holding his arm. "Hey kid, what's the problem?" called Darius. "Come here, what's up?" The child looked up briefly and then went back to crying. "COME HERE," ordered Darius. That brought action. The child rose to his feet and slowly approached Darius, who had left his clipboard and rescue tube and was now standing on deck. Darius took a look at the child's arm and saw a large lump on the outside of the elbow joint. When he asked the child to move the arm around, the child complied but cried harder, saying he had landed on his arm on the ladder when he slipped while climbing out. "Buck up," said Darius. "It's just a bruise. Go ahead and get back in." But the child replied, "I can't move my arm." "Then get out and go home" was Darius' response. The child did just that, and Darius didn't see him back at the pool for over two months. One of the other kids said the child really didn't slip and fall, but rather landed on the ladder after a long leap from the board. Why was he out for two months? His arm was in a cast after surgery to put pins into his smashed elbow.

The error list for this scenario should include the following mistakes:

- Preopening safety checklist was not done before opening.
- Lifeguard was doing paperwork while on duty.
- Child was running on deck.
- Child jumped diagonally off diving board.
- Lifeguard was not watching water.
- Lifeguard did not activate EAP when leaving stand.
- Lifeguard asked child to come to him, rather than going to injured child.
- Lifeguard asked child to move his arm when fracture would be suspected.
- Lifeguard sent child home when first aid was needed.

...continued

- No accident report was completed.
- No check was made of ladder to see if a hazard resulted in the supposed fall.
- No check was made to see if diving board was mounted too close to wall or ladder.

VARIATIONS

- Vary the activity by changing the content of the scenario. Try to use scenarios that are appropriate to your program or facility.
- Use the same scenario with several small groups of three or four participants. Challenge the groups to see who can list the most errors.

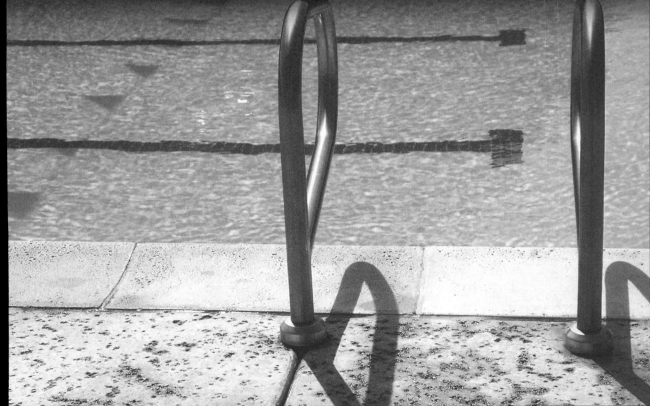

6

Team-Building Activities

Teamwork is more than a group of people participating together to accomplish a task. In the context of emergency response, teamwork means much more. Teamwork means doing all of the following:

- Anticipating what other members of the team will need in order to accomplish their part of the response
- Accommodating one's response to constantly changing situational circumstances
- Taking into account the strengths and weaknesses of other team members and adjusting personal actions to complement the work of others
- Being able to take the initiative and lead, as well as be a strong contributor as a follower
- Putting aside personal differences to work with any first responder
- Monitoring the efforts of the team, as well as one's own performance, to ensure quality results
- Respecting the efforts of all team members, even when the result is not what was anticipated
- Being able to replicate team performance in a variety of unpredictable situations
- Sharing praise as well as responsibility for failure
- Helping team members to be as good as they can be, while continuing to perfect one's own knowledge and skills
- Being able to subvert one's own desires in deference to a common goal
- Understanding and valuing how several small actions contribute to the accomplishment of a larger task
- Brainstorming to find the best solution to any problem
- Accepting constructive criticism from team members, as well as being able to give criticism in a constructive manner
- Maintaining optimal effort until all members of the team believe the task is completed

The activities and games in this chapter contribute to team building in two ways. First, they place lifeguards in situations where successful completion of a task demands more than individual effort. Most lifeguards have probably used teamwork when playing sports. However, rewards such as grades in school or a job salary have most likely been the result of individual effort.

Participating as a member of an emergency response team may be a lifeguard's first experience with the teamwork concept outside of sports. The reward of saving a life carries an entirely different meaning from earning a grade or salary. Saving a life cannot be quantified or compared to any other results-oriented activity. The activities in this chapter focus on a nonsport team task; the reward is the successful completion of the task—valued in and of itself—rather than a win, a grade, or a salary.

Team-building or cooperative activities should be structured to allow everyone to continue participating as long as possible. Everyone's contribution, no matter how small, is valued. Strive to keep everyone involved; no person should be eliminated because of inadequate performance. However, negative consequences are appropriate. Negative consequences for performance that is less than optimal will help prepare lifeguards for recertification challenges where the participants will lose certification unless their performance is nearly perfect.

Possible consequences for less-than-optimal performance during team-building activities might include engaging in additional practice of a skill that was unsuccessful or performing additional physical conditioning. Inappropriate consequences for less-than-optimal performance include hazing, corporal punishment, personal accusation, and shaming by activity leaders or fellow team members. These types of behaviors have no place in any lifeguard program. Consequences should always be something that contributes to future development and team success. Although consequences should not necessarily be fun, they should have some productive value.

If elimination is used during an activity or game, that elimination should not mean elimination from the water. Some activities can lead to swimmer elimination, but once a swimmer is eliminated, she should have something else productive to do in the pool. Appropriate elimination tasks might include the following:

- Moving to another area of the pool to practice a different skill
- Moving to another area of the pool for conditioning activities
- Starting a different game or activity
- Acting as interference for the continuing activity, thus increasing the challenge for more skilled swimmers

Some experienced lifeguards may find it difficult to work with different teams. They may prefer to work with the team they originally trained with. But team composition changes over time, as new lifeguards are hired and others move on. Even the daily operations of using substitutes and rotating stations will involve changes in team composition. The following activities involve working with everyone.

BUOY BALL TRANSPORT

EQUIPMENT   One large buoy ball (a large cage ball may be substituted) for each group of four or five participants

DESCRIPTION   Divide participants into groups of four or five persons. Each team should assume a position in deep water, next to the deck. Place a buoy ball on the deck next to each team. On a predetermined signal, the team must raise the buoy ball into the air, keeping it from touching the surface of the water. Once the buoy ball is above water, the team must work together to transport the buoy ball across the pool without letting it touch the surface. The ball must be supported without the use of any attached ropes or tethers. If the ball touches the water, the team must return to the start and begin again.

VARIATIONS

- Reduce the number of people supporting the buoy ball.
- Specify the type of stroke to be used during transport.
- Time the transport.
- Allow one person from each team to act as a wave or turbulence generator, thus increasing the difficulty for the individuals doing the transport. When generating turbulence, a person is not allowed to touch another participant or any of the buoy balls.

CANCAN LINE

EQUIPMENT None

DESCRIPTION Participants line up in a single line across one end of the pool. Each participant places a hand on the shoulder of the person on each side of him. Once all hands are in place, the entire line starts to jog or cancan kick to the opposite end of the pool. This should be a water jog, not a swim. Each person should keep his body in a vertical position. As the line crosses out of shallow water into deep water, everyone should continue to water jog until the entire line reaches the opposite end of the pool. The longer the distance to be jogged in deep water, the more difficult this task will be and the more

teamwork will be required. Participants should try to avoid pushing down on adjacent participants for support. They should also avoid jogging ahead and pulling others through the activity. Everyone should work to maintain a perfectly straight line throughout the activity—just like a cancan dance line.

VARIATIONS
- Have participants perform this entire activity in deep water.
- Allow every other participant in the line to remain motionless, keeping their legs together and still, and their arms in position as described. These individuals will be carried by the rest of the line. Again, everyone should work to maintain a perfectly straight line.
- Allow participants to place their hands on their neighbor's head (instead of on the shoulders).

IT'S YOUR JOB

EQUIPMENT   One set of job description cards per team; one scenario description per team

DESCRIPTION   This activity is designed to assist all employees in understanding and valuing the jobs of all other employees at the facility. Therefore, for maximum team-building impact, employees in all types of work positions should participate. This might include lifeguards, locker room attendants, janitorial staff, administrators, reception and office personnel, vendors, and volunteers.

Before the activity, prepare job description cards. You will need one complete set of job description cards for each participating team. A job description card contains a job title and a two- or three-sentence description of the duties of that person in the event of an emergency (see illustrations).

Women's Locker Room Attendant

Supervise locker room and hand out towels. In case of an emergency, assist lifeguards in clearing pool and deck area. Back up receptionist if needed. Assist in cleanup prior to pool reopening.

Receptionist

Answer phones, provide information, direct participants to pool check-in area. In an emergency, meet ambulance and escort EMS personnel to accident area. Coordinate location and notification of aquatic manager.

Job positions and descriptions included on these cards should be as close as possible to the actual job positions for your facility. Depending on your program staffing level, the set of job description cards might include the following positions:

- Lifeguard 1
- Lifeguard 2
- Lifeguard 3
- Locker room attendant—male
- Locker room attendant—female
- Maintenance person or janitor
- Facility manager

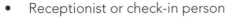

- Receptionist or check-in person
- Snack bar person
- Aquatic director
- Head lifeguard

Based on this list, a complete set of job description cards would have 11 individual cards.

Next, prepare several scenario description cards. You will need one scenario description card for each team. All teams may work on the same scenario, or a different scenario may be given to each team. A scenario description card is a card with a one- or two-sentence description of an emergency situation. Here are some typical scenario descriptions:

- Lap swimmer grasps chest, grimaces in pain, and sinks slowly to bottom.
- Child climbing out of pool slips and gashes leg on ladder rung. Leg is bleeding profusely.
- Toddler pees on pool deck.
- Lifeguard 1 does not show up for work and did not call ahead to say she was not coming in.
- Swimmer doing a back inward jackknife hits forehead on diving board.
- Teenager swimming underwater swims headfirst into pool wall. He comes up, starts to get out over the side, vomits, and collapses.

Once all materials are prepared, the group is divided into teams of six to eight people. Team assignment is random. It is not necessary to have all job categories represented on each team. Each team should appoint a team leader. The team leader distributes one job description card to each person on the team. The leader should deal the cards sight unseen, so job assignment is random. If there aren't enough job description cards for each person to have one, those participants without a card should play the role of bystanders. If there aren't enough people for all job description cards to be used, the extra cards represent positions where the staff member was a no-show that day.

Once the job description cards have been distributed, each person reads his job description from the card. Then, the team leader reads aloud the scenario description. Team participants are given five minutes to decide what their role should be during the emergency response (based on their job description card). After five minutes of thought, team members report to the group. Each team member, including the team leader, should first state his job description and then describe exactly what his role should be during the described emergency.

After individual reporting, the team leader should assist participants in looking for ways that specific job positions interact with and depend on each other. If discrepancies or disagreements occur, the chain of command for the facility takes precedence. Participants should also note how the system might break down if a key person is a no-show.

VARIATIONS   Mixing the teams frequently and redrawing for job descriptions will provide variety. The activity may also be combined with role playing; the participants actually act out the appropriate tasks to fulfill their job descriptions.

JOB TRADE

EQUIPMENT   None

DESCRIPTION   Job Trade is an activity where two people actually swap jobs for a day or a shift. Everyone's job description is put into a hat, and each person draws a different job. No, you won't be turning the lifeguard duties at your pool over to untrained individuals. However, someone who is a lifeguard can perform maintenance, work reception, staff the locker room, or perform other tasks not related to lifeguarding. By the same token, any person who is not a lifeguard can assume the position of a deck supervisor; the person would be assigned a specific location and would have surveillance over a specific portion of water. *The surveillance provided by this person is in addition to that provided by on-duty lifeguards.* This person would NOT respond to an in-water emergency, but the person could alert lifeguards and perform other duties to assist in an emergency. For this activity, the entire staff does not need to switch jobs on the same day. If two people switch each week, by the end of a term or season, everyone will have experienced a job other than her own. This is a great way to help staff members understand the contribution that each person makes to the successful running of an aquatic program.

VARIATIONS   Add a discussion format to the job exchange. This will give participants a chance to express feelings about their new job, as well as to compliment the person who must usually perform that job. During job trades, you may need to provide additional staff in order to make sure the integrity of facility operations is not compromised. Note: This activity is also a way to help all staff members learn how to cover different positions for times when there is a staff shortage.

KNOTS

EQUIPMENT   None

DESCRIPTION   Standing in waist-deep water, participants form a circle. Once the circle is formed, all participants walk into the center of the circle and extend both arms. Next, each person grasps the hands of someone else. A person should not grasp hands with the person on either side of her. Each person should grasp hands with two other people, giving her right hand to one person and her left hand to a different person. Once all participants have grasped hands, a knot has been formed. Then the group task is to untangle that knot, reforming the original circle (but with different individuals to either side of each person).

In untangling the knot, several rules apply:

- Hands must remain grasped.
- Hands cannot be let go and then regrasped to facilitate untangling.
- Hands may be temporarily released to adjust swimsuits.

VARIATIONS

- Perform the activity with all participants blindfolded and one person on deck giving untangling directions.
- Divide the group into two teams. Each team makes a knot, and on a start signal, the teams race to see which group can untangle its knot the quickest.

RESCUE BOARD PUSH-UPS

EQUIPMENT   One rescue board for every four people; one plastic glass

DESCRIPTION   Participants are divided into teams of four people. Each team places its rescue board in deep water; two people are positioned on each long side of the board. A glass filled with water is placed in the center of the board. Each person must perform one full push-up on the edge of the rescue board. As one person does a push-up, the other three individuals must counterbalance the board so it remains flat and stable. The object is for all four individuals—in whatever order they choose—to each perform one push-up on the board without the glass of water tipping over.

VARIATIONS

- Set a specific amount of time that the push-up must be held in the up position.
- Add a fifth person to each team. After doing a push-up, the person must drop off and swim to the opposite side of the board. This will force the team to do push-ups on alternating sides of the board.
- Set a maximum number of seconds allowed between each individual push-up.
- Ask participants to wear sweatshirts, thus increasing the weight lifted on the push-up and making the balance task more difficult.

RESCUE RELAY

EQUIPMENT   Whistle; rescue equipment as determined by the type of rescue staged in the activity

DESCRIPTION   Participants are divided into two teams. Each team chooses one person to be the victim. The victims enter the water and assume positions dictated by the rescue situation being used. The rest of the team members line up single file, one behind the other, at one end of the pool. The first person in line is considered the lifeguard on duty. When the victim initiates the scenario by acting out his victim role, the lifeguard on duty activates the EAP and enters the water to make the appropriate rescue. While the rescue is in progress, you blow your whistle and call "relay." When relay is called, the next person in line (now in the "lifeguard on duty" position) must take up the rescue from whatever point the starting lifeguard is at. For example, if the first responding lifeguard is swimming and is halfway to the victim, the second participant in the relay enters the water, swims to the point where the first participant is located, and takes the place of the first participant. The second responding lifeguard continues the rescue from that point. The first responding lifeguard leaves the rescue area, returns to deck, and takes a place at the end of the relay line.

Blow your whistle (signaling a relay exchange) several times during the rescue scenario. Depending on the type of rescue, this might be during the swim out, during body retrieval, during backboard placement, during backboard strap down, during victim carry, during lift out, during resuscitation, or during first aid. No matter when the whistle is blown, the next lifeguard in line picks up the rescue from that point. Tell participants that the exchange should be made with as little endangerment to the victim as possible—in the same way such an exchange might have to be made if the first rescuer was unable to complete the rescue.

VARIATIONS
- This activity does not need to be competitive. However, the activity could be scored based on the effectiveness of the lifeguard exchanges. It could also be scored based on the amount of time taken to complete the rescue. With two teams going at the same time, the teams might not be at the same point when the whistle is sounded.
- You should vary the type of rescue situation used (e.g., active victim, double drowning, spinal injury, unresponsive and nonbreathing victim, submerged victim, or a victim needing first aid for severe bleeding or suspected fractures).

SHAKE OUT

EQUIPMENT   One canoe; one watch with a second hand (or a stopwatch)

DESCRIPTION   Divide participants into pairs or teams. The length of the canoe will determine the number of people on a team. A 17-foot (5.2 m) canoe can function with teams of four or five. A shorter canoe can have teams of three or four. All team members enter the canoe and hand-paddle out into the middle of the deep end of the pool. On a predetermined signal, the timer starts keeping time, and the team members swamp their canoe. Once the canoe is totally swamped, the team's task is to shake out the canoe until there is no water in the craft. When the team has almost all of the water out, they may need to have someone enter the canoe and use his hands to bail the remaining water. When the canoe is totally empty, all team members reboard the canoe (from deep water) and hand-paddle back to the start. Time stops when the canoe reaches the starting point. If the canoe tips again while participants are entering from deep water, the whole process must start again. Each team tries to complete the activity in the fastest time.

VARIATIONS   You may or may not want to give participants hints on how to accomplish the task. If giving clues on how to shake out the canoe, advise the teams to position team members on opposite sides of the craft. Advise the group to work together using alternating gunnel rocking to shake out enough water so the rest can be bailed by hand.

TEAM PARACHUTE

EQUIPMENT   One parachute (the parachute can have handles or not); additional equipment as described in the variations

DESCRIPTION   Because of its size and shape, a parachute is ideal for activities that help participants develop teamwork. When selecting a parachute, choose a size that allows the parachute to be spread out on the surface of the water with at least a full lane of space between any edge of the chute and any pool wall. Also consider the number of people in the group. The more participants, the larger the parachute should be. A parachute can be used for activities in shallow water—in which case, the activities will be similar to parachute activities on land. If you take that parachute into deep water and perform many of the same activities, an extremely challenging situation is created. In deep water, participants must have strong supporting kicks. Caution: When working with a parachute in the pool, watch carefully to be sure no one becomes trapped under the parachute as it rests on the water surface.

VARIATIONS   A variety of parachute activities can be used for lifeguard training. Some of these activities are described in the following sections.

Parachute Tug-of-War

Spread the parachute on the surface of the water; the chute should be as centered in the activity area as possible. Have participants gather (evenly spaced) around the parachute, grasping the parachute in both hands. Divide the group across the center, making two teams. The two teams have their backs to opposite walls of the pool. On a given signal, each team should attempt to pull the other team until the wall behind the pulling team is reached. This can be a single pull competition or a best-of-several series of pulls. Caution: Prearrange a stop signal to use in case a team gets too close to a non-goal wall. To vary this activity, specify the kick to be used during the pull. You could also allow participants to hold the parachute with only one hand and use the other to aid in the swim. Another option is to use rescue tubes; participants grasp the parachute by reaching over the tube (similar to carrying a victim).

...continued

Ball Bounce

Spread the parachute on the surface of the water; the chute should be as centered in the activity area as possible. Have participants gather (evenly spaced) around the parachute, grasping the parachute in both hands. Place several inflated balls on the center of the parachute. By alternately lifting and lowering the parachute, participants try to get as many balls lifted into the air at the same time as possible. To vary this activity, participants can try to loft balls into the air and off the parachute over the head of someone else. At the same time, each participant should try to prevent any balls from flying off the parachute over his own head. One point is scored each time a ball flies over the head of a participant—the winner is the participant with the lowest point total.

Transport

Spread the parachute on the surface of the water, with one edge next to a side wall of the pool. Have participants gather (evenly spaced) around the parachute, grasping the parachute in both hands. One participant is selected to be the rider. The rider crawls onto the parachute and moves to the center. To make the parachute a stable platform, those around the chute must pull back as hard as they can, making the chute taunt. Once the rider is centered on the chute, the group must move the rider to the opposite side without the rider getting wet. Participants around the side may gather up as much of the chute as necessary to create a flat platform. To vary this activity, allow participants to provide additional support from under the parachute, holding the chute and the body of the rider above the water surface.

Speed Ride

Spread the parachute on the surface of the water at one side of the activity area. Have participants gather (evenly spaced) around the parachute, grasping the parachute in both hands. Divide the group across the center, making two teams. The two teams have their backs to opposite walls of the pool. On a given signal, the team farthest away from the wall starts to pull and continues to pull until they reach the opposite side of the pool. The team starting close to the wall does nothing but hang on to the parachute. Time is started as soon as the starting signal is given, and time stops when the first person touches the opposite side.

Note the time. When the touch is made and the time is noted, the timer should call "reverse." On the reverse call, the riding team starts to pull, and the pulling team rides back to where they started. The new pulling team tries to beat the time of the first pull across. This sequence continues, with teams alternating the pull across, each trying to beat the time of the previous team. You can vary this activity by specifying the kick to be used. Also, rescue tubes can be added for each participant in the holding position; each person must reach over the tube to grasp the parachute. Another option is to have participants perform this activity moving through a course of tethered floating obstacles.

7

Special Activities

Special activities are those that do not fit into the traditional categories for lifeguard training. Rather, they are activities that originated in some other discipline—aquatic or not—and are easily adapted for use in aquatic training. These special activities provide unique ways of helping lifeguards achieve and maintain a high level of fitness and performance.

Aqua Square Dance originated in the fields of dance and social interaction. Performed in deep water, Aqua Square Dance is continuous choreographed movement without assistance of any buoyant aids. Aqua Square Dance can augment any conditioning program, and it helps lifeguards learn to focus on following directions while also interacting with fellow participants. You, too, can lead Aqua Square Dance. This chapter details how to do it.

Aqua step originated in the field of physical fitness with step aerobics. Aquatic exercise professionals recognized that this cardio activity could also be done in water. The development of a step platform that was appropriate for use in the water made the activity possible. Your lifeguards can reap the benefits of aqua step conditioning, and this chapter will get you started.

Challenge testing originated in the field of education. Performed on land as well as in water, challenge testing is an extremely efficient method of recertification. To prepare for challenge testing, lifeguards must learn the appropriate concepts and skills. In addition, the lifeguards must adjust their attitude to conform to the structure of having to achieve a high standard of performance—rather than just exert effort—in order to achieve success. This chapter will assist you in helping your lifeguards make the transition to the proper mind-set for performance-based testing.

Field experiences also originated in the field of education. Field experiences expand the learning environment from the classroom and pool to actual community settings related to emergency response. Lifeguards learn how other professional rescuers accomplish their jobs. The lifeguards also develop skills for bridging the gap between the care provided by on-site first responders (the lifeguards themselves) and the arrival of responding professional rescuers from ambulance companies and hospitals.

Fitness testing originated in the disciplines of health and physical education. Lifeguard programs must include physical conditioning. Fitness testing provides feedback to the individual lifeguard, as well as the lifeguard manager, regarding whether or not that program is meeting the needs of participants. The Ball State 500-Yard Water Run is included here as a standardized fitness measure.

Holiday celebration originated in the area of social psychology. People need to have pleasant social interactions with each other. The more stressful the job, the stronger the need to provide opportunities to relax, release tension, and create positive social bonds with one's peers. Celebrating holidays and other special events can provide those opportunities. This chapter provides some good ideas on how to do this.

Journaling originated in the fields of communications and language arts. We write to express ourselves, to help us think through decision making, and to share our thoughts and emotions. Journaling can help lifeguards process meaningful events, such as life-and-death situations, as well as difficult training circumstances. Ways to include journaling in your lifeguarding program are presented here.

Junior guard activities originated in the apprenticeship programs of the trades. Younger workers learned from those more highly skilled. Effective junior guard activities can help ensure that you'll have a continual supply of qualified lifeguards for your facility. This chapter will assist you in developing this type of lifeguard feeder system.

Lifeguard competitions originated in the Olympics of olden days, when warriors competed to determine the more skilled warrior. For lifeguards who spend most of their time sitting on a stand, a lifeguard competition provides a great opportunity to sharpen skills. Competitions also encourage lifeguards to take pride in maintaining that high degree of skill necessary for optimal emergency response. This chapter includes the basics that any aquatic manager needs to know in order to organize a lifeguard competition.

Polka Jog originated in the combined disciplines of dance, social interaction, and physical fitness. The dance and social interaction aspects of Polka Jog provide a pleasant experience, motivated by music. Physical fitness is enhanced through the continuous activity against resistance. You can include a brief Polka Jog session in any lifeguard training session. You may also schedule a longer, more strenuous Polka Jog as a full water workout.

Relays originated in our early communication systems, as messengers worked in relays to spread information. Because speed was paramount, it was not long before relays were staged solely to determine the fastest team or group. Many of the activities and games in this book can be adapted to a relay format. This chapter explains how.

Timed events have been with us as long as we have been able to measure time. We wonder how long something will take, when someone will arrive, or whether one is faster than another. In emergency response, time is a critical factor, often meaning the difference between life and death. Adding a time factor to a lifeguarding activity or game can call attention to the need for quick response and can motivate lifeguards to be as time efficient as possible in all they do. This chapter describes how to add the time factor to your training.

There is no single activity or game that is perfect for all lifeguard training. The greater variety you can build into training, the more all aspects of lifeguard performance will be enhanced. Unexpected changes in training content will keep lifeguards focused and engaged in activities, not only providing motivation for performance, but also increasing their enjoyment of training.

AQUA SQUARE DANCE

Elbow swing round and round.
Now promenade around the town.
Change direction, go the other way.
Listen well, heed what I say.
Now do-si-do another friend, and
Two-hand swing around again!

A barn dance? Maybe a country social event? Guess again, it's a high-intensity pool workout, guaranteed to get heart rates up and smiles on faces. It's Aqua Square Dance! Take the music of traditional square dance, add your own calls, put it in the pool, and you have a high-intensity workout. Lifeguards sometimes need a break but can't afford to take a training day off. Something totally different, such as Aqua Square Dance, can provide a great workout while breaking that training boredom.

WATER Taking square dance into the pool makes for quite a workout. Moving against the resistance of the water is not easy. The beat of the music keeps everyone going. Even when the dance calls for some dancers to stay in place while others are moving, the dancers staying in place can mark time, jog, or tread in place. No one's feet or legs should ever be still. In Aqua Square Dance, movement is constant.

Water depth, in part, determines the difficulty or intensity of the workout. Aqua Square Dance can be done in any depth of water. Obviously, the easiest is in waist-deep water. The most difficult is in deep water with no buoyant support. Participants must then tread throughout the activity. The dance can also be done in chest-deep water. Lifeguards should be able to Aqua Square Dance easily in deep water.

Frequent changes in the direction of movement during dances also make for increased difficulty. Moving against a current created by other dancers—as well as changing from in-place action to locomotor action—adds to the intensity. Keeping up with the calls also requires increased efforts.

No matter what water depth the dance is performed in, participants should maintain a reasonably vertical position. Appropriate locomotor action is walking, jogging, running, or treading. A vertical position keeps an individual's feet

Adapted from S. Grosse, 2002, " Swing and promenade for heart rate high," *AKWA* 15(6): 12-14.

under the trunk, where they are less likely to kick another person who may be in close proximity. Participants in Aqua Square Dance should not swim or move in a horizontal position. For safety, caution participants to be careful to avoid kicking other swimmers during close dance maneuvers.

Participants can use their arms to aid locomotion, unless the arms are used in an action itself. For example, during an elbow swing, the outside arm (the one that is not hooked) can be used to help pull so the dancers move in a circle. However, in a do-si-do, both arms should remain across the chest.

CALLS   Traditional square dance calls are easily adapted to Aqua Square Dance. The most universal change is in the tempo of the calls. Locomotor movement through water takes more time than that same movement on land. Therefore, calls should be paced to the performance of participants. A general rule to follow is to give a call and then wait (or put in vocal patter) until participants have almost completed an action. When the participants are more than halfway to the finish of one specific action, you should start the next call. That way, aqua dancers move from one action directly into the next.

Different groups will need different pacing. Stronger dancers complete actions sooner; weaker participants are a lot slower. You should pace the calls for the group as a whole. Several actions that may be put into a dance can continue for many repetitions. These actions allow slower individuals to catch up, while also keeping stronger aqua dancers moving.

For Aqua Square Dance, a second modification that may be needed is changing gender-related calls to neutral calls. Square dance is traditionally called for ladies and gentlemen or girls and guys. Aquatic groups are rarely coed to the extent that each participant can have a partner of the opposite sex. The generic term *partner* can be substituted, or partners can become 1s and 2s or As and Bs. For some aqua dances, it won't matter at all. For calls with more complicated figures, having one partner be a shark and the other partner be a ray will simplify the calls.

A third modification for calls is the elimination of any square formations. Although it is possible to use square formations in this activity (with four partner pairs in each square), doing so is not necessary. A random scatter of partner pairs works just fine. These partner pairs can move in and out of formations as needed. Formations can be built directly into the calls so that moving in and out of formations becomes part of the exercise.

The calls determine the actions of participants—henceforth called dancers! The call tells the dancer exactly what to do. As the caller, you speak the call, trying to speak in time to the rhythm of the music. Dancers hear the call and then perform the action. A call can be any physical action. Being creative is good. This will keep dancers listening and thinking. Begin with easy calls and progress to more complicated ones.

Basic Calls

- Salutation and bow
- Elbow swing
- Two-hand swing

...continued

- Promenade
- Do-si-do
- Circle left and right
- In to the center

Advanced Calls

- Find a new partner
- Make an arch
- Dip and dive
- Corner or neighbor
- Circle 4, 6, 8
- Texas Star

Each call has a specific action. After giving the call itself, provide as much initial direction as needed to facilitate participants following the call (see table 7.1).

Table 7.1 Aqua Square Dance Call and Action

Call	Action
Honor your partner	This is a salutation or greeting. It can be a bow, a nod of the head, or a smile and a wave. It is given with partners facing each other, or facing whomever they are honoring.
Swing your partner	Partners face each other, hook right elbows, and move in a circle around each other.
Two-hand swing your partner	Partners face each other, join hands, and circle around each other.
Left elbow swing	Partners face each other, hook left elbows, and move in a circle around each other.
Promenade	Partners position themselves side by side, facing the same direction, and they join inside hands. Then they lift their joined hands above water, and the partners water jog forward together.
Do-si-do	Partners face each other and cross their arms across their own chests. Then they move toward each other, passing right shoulders. As soon as the partners are past each other, they both move sideward into a back-to-back position. From the back-to-back position, each partner backs up to her starting position and drops her arms.
Circle left and right	All dancers join hands in a circle. Once connected, the circle turns to the called direction.
In to the center	This is done from a circle formation. All dancers face the center and water jog forward until the circle is as small as it can get. Once in the center, the dancers can be directed to "give a yell," "share a high-five," or move "back to the bar" (their original position).

Call	Action
Find a new partner	At any point, it can be advantageous to change partners. The easiest way to facilitate this is to call for action with a new partner, as in "two-hand swing a new person." When this happens, established partners release. Each goes to a different person, and the called action continues. The new partner is now the person's established partner, and dancers do not go back to a previous partner.
Make an arch	One pair of dancers face each other, joining both hands. They then raise their joined hands as high as possible out of the water and overhead. Making an arch is preliminary to having the rest of the group promenade under that arch.
Dip and dive	Dip and dive is what promenading partners do when they go under an arch.
Corner or neighbor	Sometimes dancers make a temporary change of partners. If dancing in a square, a person's partner dances on one side of him; the person on the other side of him is referred to as his corner. If dancers are not dancing in a square, it is easier to refer to a different, temporary partner as a neighbor. In effect, a neighbor is the next closest person. After an action with a neighbor or corner, the next call usually returns a person to his established partner. Here's an example: "Right elbow swing your neighbor. Then, go back home and swing your partner."
Circle 4, 6, and 8	This is a variation of a circle formation. The call tells dancers how many people should make up the circle. The usual progression is to move from partners to a circle of 4, from a circle of 4 to a circle of 6 or 8, and then on to a large circle with the whole group. Circles of different sizes create different turbulence patterns; therefore, each circle is challenging in its own way.
Texas Star	For this formation, each person in a partner pair needs to have an individual designation. In regular square dance on land, this would be ladies and gents. In Aqua Square Dance, pairings are random, so designations must be free of gender specificity. Sharks and rays, As and Bs, and 1s and 2s are all designations that work fine. The call for Texas Star begins with dancers in a circle formation. Then directions are given as follows: "Sharks to the center and back to the bar. Rays to the center and form a star." First, the sharks go forward into the middle of the circle and then back up to their original positions. When the sharks are back in place, the rays go forward, and each ray extends her right arm and hand to touch the hands of all the other rays. This forms a right-hand star. Then the star turns. Each ray makes a quarter turn left; then, with all hands still touching, the rays travel forward, turning the star in a wheel while the sharks remain in place. When it is time to break the star, the following call is made: "Let that star in the heavens whirl. Go back home and give your partner a twirl." The star continues to turn until each ray is back to her partner shark. On meeting, the partners swing.

...continued

Some calls are very self-descriptive. Dancers know what to do from what is said. Other calls, such as Texas Star, are more complicated to understand when doing them for the first time. In this case, the caller may give additional directions after each call. For example, during Texas Star, directions could be added as follows:

Sharks to the center and back to the bar.

Okay, Sharks, face the center and go all the way in.

Now go back to your places, Sharks.

Rays to the center and form a star.

Rays, it's your turn now. Go in to the middle, put out your right hand.

Yes, touch hands with those other rays. Now face left and turn your star.

Give as much direction as needed. You may even call specific dancers by name if someone appears really confused or lost in the activity.

Creativity starts when the caller inserts calls such as "wiggle your ears" or "left ankle swing." These are obviously not traditional square dance movements, but they can be added to an Aqua Square Dance in order to generate challenging movement as well as some humor.

Any calls can be mixed and repeated to create dances (see example 1 in table 7.2). For dances containing more complex figures, such as the Texas Star, additional calls can be added to begin or end the dance or to act as breaks within the dance (see example 2).

Table 7.2 Texas Star Example

Example 1—Warm-up	Example 2—Texas Star
Honor your partner.	Honor your partner.
Greet your neighbor.	Greet your neighbor.
Swing your partner.	Swing your partner and promenade.
Swing your neighbor.	Gather up 6 and circle left.
Do-si-do your partner.	Sharks to the center and back to the bar.
Promenade (tell partners they can promenade anywhere in deep water).	Rays to the center and form a star.
Two-hand swing your partner.	Let that star in the heavens whirl; go back home and give your partner a twirl.
Two-hand swing your neighbor.	Swing your partner round and round, then promenade all around the town.
Left elbow swing your partner.	Swing your neighbor high and low, keep this one, and home you go. (Each person gets a new partner; preferably, sharks get rays and vice versa. However, if two sharks get each other, one partner can just change roles.)
Left elbow swing your neighbor.	
Promenade.	
(Repeat from call "Swing your partner.")	
Bow to your partner.	(Repeat the dance from call "Swing your partner and neighbor.")
Wave to all your neighbors—say "bye."	Do-si-do for one last time.
	Wave to your neighbors, you did fine.

Notice that the Texas Star dance becomes a mixer—dancers swing their neighbor and then keep that person to repeat the dance. Partners can also change if the star breaks up with the call "Let that star in the heavens whirl, go past your partner and give the next one a twirl." Part of the fun in square dance is that dancers must listen for calls, because the caller can be unpredictable! Square dance books and records are good sources for calls and figures, but it is just as easy to make them up from scratch.

MUSIC Although Aqua Square Dance can be done without music, dancers will find it much easier to keep up the pace when a musical beat is provided. Traditional square dance music works just fine without modifications. Use music that does not include prerecorded calls. Calls (directions) determine the activity to go with the music, but prerecorded calls go too fast for performing in water. You need to do your own calls. In selecting music, listen for something with a good beat and clear fiddle line, such as country music played by traditional country musical instruments—in other words, toe-tapping music. It will also help if your sound system allows you to use a microphone to give calls over the amplitude of the music.

Any square dance or country western music will work well for this activity. A great resource for beginning square dancing on land is the Honor Your Partner series (a series of six CDs). Each CD has about six dances; each dance is presented in two versions. One version is a talk-through and walk-through—the CD teaches the group the dance as the dancers visualize what is being explained. The second version is a called ver-

sion of the dance. You may use the calls from the CD to call the same dance yourself (to square dance music—as in music only, no recorded calls); that way you can pace the dance to the speed of the dancers.

...continued

AQUA SQUARE DANCE AND LIFEGUARDING   In Aqua Square Dance, the focus is on performing dances as called. This shifts focus from the intensity of activity to the fun of accomplishments. Group interactions, particularly as partners work together to complete calls, result in plenty of smiles and good-natured laughter. Aqua Square Dance can be a fun break from the day's activity, as well as a way to add variety to your high-intensity workouts.

AQUA STEP

Long a favorite of aquatic exercise classes, aqua step can provide variety and a good workout for your lifeguards. Step aerobics in the pool is very similar to step aerobics outside the pool. Put your stepping platforms into the water, turn on the music, and step.

The basic benefit of aqua stepping is cardiorespiratory conditioning. The more shallow the water, the greater the amount of effort needed to step. In very shallow water, stepping almost approximates step aerobics on land. In deeper water, buoyancy assists and the person stepping carries less weight in the process. Each participant can choose his water depth based on individual needs. Someone wanting a more strenuous workout might select knee- or hip-depth water. A participant who is healing after an ankle, knee, or hip injury might need to perform in shoulder-depth water. Even if starting in deeper water, a person can place his step in gradually shallower water as conditioning or healing occurs.

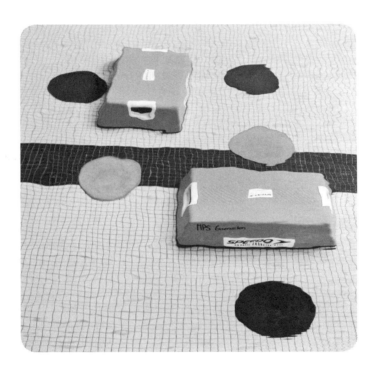

EQUIPMENT   Basic to aqua stepping is the aqua step platform. Several companies make a step platform designed specifically for use in water. Aqua steps are made out of material heavy enough to sink and stay on the bottom—while still being easy to take in and out. Aqua steps dry easily and can be stacked for storage.

In addition to the aqua step, participants will probably want to wear some form of footgear. Repeatedly stepping and pushing off from the pool bottom can result in scraped feet. Some pool bottoms can be slippery. Footgear can increase traction. Arch support is also important for activities that involve impact

...continued

on the lower extremities. Selecting a water shoe with arch support—instead of just an aqua slipper—will provide increased stability and joint cushioning, as well as improve body alignment. Whatever the shoe, the foot should fit comfortably into the shoe, with no points of abrasion that might cause blisters.

Depending on water depth, a participant may want to wear upper body covering. If the torso will be out of water (e.g., when working in hip-depth water), chilling may occur as water evaporates or if the individual is in a draft. Wearing a T-shirt can prevent evaporation chilling. On the other hand, if the environment is very hot and humid, evaporation may actually cool the body, minimizing sticky sweat. The body will still generate sweat, but the sweat will wash away with a cooling effect and be less noticeable than on land.

If a participant wants to increase the workload, she can wear additional clothing. Stepping while wearing a sweat suit will increase overall weight as the suit becomes water saturated. This same effect can be gained by wearing a weight belt. However, wearing a sweat suit will distribute the additional weight more evenly and have less impact on balance.

Last but not least is the music. Stepping can be done without music. However, just as walking is usually done to a cadence (even if the person does not concentrate on that cadence), so is stair climbing. That cadence is an aid to performance. Music with a beat establishes this cadence. Music also lightens the load, as a person's mind blends focus with the musical patterns of rhythm, melody, instrumentation, and vocal components. March music or other selections with 4/4 time or 2/4 time work best. A step pattern is based on right–left stepping. This makes music organized in factors of two most appropriate. Music in 3/4 time, such as a waltz, would be difficult for a beginning stepper. This music would be more appropriate for more complicated step patterns that include some movement in place between steps. Select music with a strong, but not harsh, beat. The beat should be slightly slower for warm-up and cool-down, and it should be slightly faster for the main cardio portion of the stepping workout.

STEPPING PATTERNS   Stepping is all about foot placement while stepping onto and off of the step platform. The platform functions just like a stair step—the person places a foot onto the platform, transfers weight onto that foot, straightens the weighted leg, and brings the unweighted trailing leg up alongside the first foot. Either foot can be placed first. Once both feet are on the platform, the process can be reversed to step down backward, or the participant can step down moving forward and off the opposite side of the step.

When stepping, the participant's arms can be used in a variety of ways. The easiest is to use the arms for balance and stability, alternating forward arm swings with reciprocal steps. Participants can also keep their arms at their sides or crossed across their chest. This position will require the participant to use more core strength and balance to maintain stability and keep up the pace. To increase the cardio load, arm exercise actions can be added to the stepping patterns.

Numerous variations of this basic step pattern can be used, including the following:

- Step on, step off to the side.
- Step on from the side, step off forward or backward.
- Step on, step off forward, walk around the step and repeat.

- Step on, step to the side on the platform, step to the other side on the platform, step off.
- Step on, knee slap right, knee slap left, step off.
- Step on using a diagonal step to the left, crossing right foot over left. Step off. Step on using a diagonal step to the right, crossing left foot over right. Step off.
- Reach for the sky when stepping up and down; bring the arms down to sides as the trailing foot is used.
- Add a specific arm action or exercise in time to the step cadence.
- Keep jogging arms going with each beat of the cadence.

STEPS COMBINED WITH OTHER ACTIVITIES   Aqua step can be used as an individual activity or combined with another activity format. For example, aqua steps can be placed across the path of travel for Polka Jog (the shallow-water portions of the path) or included in a poly trail. Now jogging participants will also have to jog up and over the aqua steps as they proceed around the jogging path. Aqua steps can also be added to any shallow-water relay, forcing participants to step up and over as they work to accomplish tasks.

AQUA STEP DURATION   How long should an aqua step workout be? It can be as long as you want it to be. Aqua step can be a warm-up, an addition to a longer activity, or an entire workout session. The duration will depend on the goals for the workout, as well as the general condition of participants. It is possible to monitor exertion by taking a pulse or by using a perceived exertion scale. However, the easiest method to use in an aquatic format is the talk test. If your participants can still carry on a conversation, they have not reached maximum exertion.

CHALLENGE TESTING

Most national-level training programs include a challenge format for credentialing. Information provided here is not meant to take the place of the challenge guidelines of any national program. Rather, this information is intended to facilitate the challenge process and assist aquatic managers in implementing successful challenge opportunities for lifeguard staff.

CHALLENGE FORMAT   Challenge is a testing format in which participants are expected to know all material to be tested. A challenge format session contains only testing. There is no instruction. There is no video viewing, skill practice, coaching, error correction, open-book assistance, peer consultation, or any other assistance provided. Retries of failed items are rarely allowed. The passing standard for written tests is usually at least 80 percent, with no retest.

This type of format means that participants in challenge testing must prepare ahead of time. Very few individuals can succeed in a challenge without any previous practice or study. Success at challenge testing demands a high degree of advance preparation.

CHALLENGE PROBLEMS   A variety of problems can result in unsuccessful participation in challenge testing. Here are some common problems:

- Lack of preparation by the challenging lifeguard. The lifeguard is not ready or prepared to challenge.
- Lack of understanding of the challenge format. The lifeguard does not understand that he will not receive assistance or coaching during testing.
- Inconsistent administration of challenge testing. The person administering the testing does not apply the rules of the challenge test format appropriately or consistently. Therefore, participants are not sure what to expect.
- Inappropriate procedures by testing staff. The person administering the testing purposely assists the challenge participant. This is also called cheating. When one lifeguard passes a challenge based on cheating, this lifeguard and others learn to expect a cheating assist.
- Failure to allow sufficient time to accomplish a complete challenge. Some challenge formats stipulate the amount of time required for a challenge or stipulate that all challenge testing must occur in a single time period.
- Failure of participants to realize the consequences. Participants do not really believe they will not credential if they fail a challenge, or they do not believe it is possible for them to fail a challenge if they try hard.

FACILITATING CHALLENGES   In spite of the aforementioned problems, challenge is an exceptionally efficient method of testing. Lifeguards who are familiar with the challenge process can learn how to prepare for challenge testing and can come through the process with a high degree of success. These lifeguards will also be the most highly skilled and knowledgeable guards on your staff.

Originally published in S. Grosse, 2002, *Lifeguard training games and gimmicks* (Milwaukee, WI: Aquatic Consulting & Education Resource Services).

Here are some suggestions for implementing and maintaining a challenge format:

- Plan ahead for challenge deadlines. If there is a stipulation that currently credentialed lifeguards can challenge more than one time as long as their credential is current, schedule a challenge during that window of opportunity. Then, if a challenge is failed, there will be another opportunity to pass before a credential expires.

- Schedule regular in-service trainings on applicable skills and knowledge. Frequent practice should be part of every lifeguard employment program. Use the activities and games in this book to determine and highlight areas of strength as well as weakness. Train to maintain strengths and to remediate weaknesses.

- Become very familiar with the guidelines and procedures for implementing a challenge format within the national program credentialing your lifeguards. Challenge is more than just testing. Make sure you know the rules regarding assisting participants, number of trials, and other components of the testing process.

- Educate your lifeguards regarding the guidelines and procedures that will be used for implementing challenge testing. Particularly, explain how challenge testing will be different from initial certification testing. Provide a demonstration of a typical challenge, including an example of how you will handle errors and retries.

- Become familiar with any information provided by your national program regarding common errors in performance. Coach your lifeguards not to make those errors.

- Implement the challenge format according to national program guidelines. Even if few (or none) of your lifeguards pass a challenge the first time, after failing a challenge, the lifeguards are very unlikely to fail it a second time.

- If a challenge is failed, be prepared to provide instructional opportunities during which a lifeguard can regain her certification. This might require the lifeguard to take a review course or to retake the full lifeguard training course (if a retake of the challenge is not possible).

- Let lifeguards know that passing a challenge depends on skill and knowledge, not just showing up or saying they tried. Even the most popular lifeguard must be replaced if her credential is not current. This is not a reward they will receive for just showing up.

- Be consistent in organizing and implementing challenges. Leave no doubt in the minds of your lifeguards regarding how you will stage (and how you feel about) each and every challenge.

- Promote success at challenge testing as something all lifeguards should strive for. Add incentives for lifeguards who pass a challenge on the first try, or those who take a challenge every time it is offered (rather than just

...continued

CHALLENGE TESTING ...*continued*

when they have to). Post the names of those who challenge successfully. Publicize successful challenges. Pay lifeguards for time spent doing a successful challenge, but do not pay if that same lifeguard must retake a course.

Challenge testing takes the least amount of time to implement of all the ways to certify and recertify lifeguards. Successful challenge testing generates great pride and self-esteem. You can include challenge testing in your lifeguard program. Once in place, the challenge format will be the most popular to everyone involved.

FIELD EXPERIENCES

Field experiences place lifeguards in actual venues related to emergency response so they can have experiences as close to the real thing as can be arranged (these experiences should always include supervision and guidance from experienced emergency response personnel). Having a field experience can add a realistic perspective to the lifeguards' text learning and peer group practice. Lifeguards see training course content in action. Because lifeguard training is an ongoing process, even for certified lifeguards, the lifeguards will benefit from continual performance feedback during the experience, as well as discussions afterward.

Lifeguards who are new to a particular program or facility can particularly benefit from field experiences. The opportunity to view working situations and conditions unique to a venue or team can prove invaluable to that lifeguard when he assumes his job role. Even experienced guards can benefit from some time spent viewing performance from a different point of reference (out of the immediate action). Everyone can benefit from expanding their knowledge of risk management and emergency response.

Typical field experiences might include the following:

• Providing lifeguard surveillance or assistance during an open swim. This surveillance should be in addition to the surveillance provided by lifeguards on the job that day. The assistance might include orientations for new patrons, enforcement of pool rules, equipment management, duplication of safety checks and water chemistry analysis, and assistance during rescue efforts. This assistance should be focused. Focus points might include safety, task efficiency, public relations, time on task, professionalism, or situational appropriateness. Although a field experience lifeguard should in no way take the place of an on-the-job guard, performing some of those same tasks while still in observation mode is a valuable learning experience.

• Traveling to an open-water site to perform rescues learned or practiced only in a pool. Open-water experiences are particularly important for practice of rescues involving small craft, rescue boards, spinal injury, and submerged victims (including search). Although it is always nice if these experiences can take place on a warm, sunny day, do not avoid rescue practice in less desirable weather. Lifeguards cannot control what the weather will be like when an actual emergency occurs. Even if these are not rescues that might be used at your facility, when it comes time for your lifeguards to renew their certifications, the knowledge and skills perfected during this type of field experience can be important to the recertification process.

• Traveling to a camp setting to assess camp waterfront facilities and operations, review small craft arrangements, and learn more about aquatic jobs in camp settings. Summer means camp jobs are numerous. This opens the potential for sharing lifeguard staff. Preparing lifeguards for camp waterfront work can be an important addition to your lifeguard training program.

• Traveling to a water park (indoor or outdoor) to assess water park operations, park duties of lifeguards, and the management procedures specific to water parks. Even if you have no water park activities at your facility, with the

...continued

current growth in popularity of these types of activities, many standard pools are adding slides and other water play equipment. This will necessitate additional training for lifeguards.

- Visiting a local ambulance company or inviting these professional rescuers to bring a rig to your facility. Lifeguards are first responders in the chain of care, and they must be able to interface well with other rescue personnel. In addition, lifeguards need to learn how specialized rescues, such as deep-water spinal injury rescues and backboarding, will be handled. A coordinated approach to victim care will result in improved outcomes for victims.

- Visiting the emergency department of a local hospital. Just as knowing more about the tasks of ambulance personnel is important, lifeguards can also benefit from knowing how drowning victims are cared for when they reach the hospital. This type of experience helps the lifeguards better understand the impact of the care they provide, as well as the teamwork necessary for effective victim care.

FITNESS TESTING

Fitness testing on land is familiar to everyone. Fitness testing in the pool opens additional opportunities for assessing cardiorespiratory fitness and monitoring progress made in conditioning. The Ball State Water Run has been proven to correlate highly with the 1.5-mile land run (Robbins, 1993, p. 9). It can be used for individuals age 14 to 30. Participants can test to determine cardiorespiratory fitness at any given time, and they can retest at monthly intervals to assess progress. Administering the test and scoring is relatively easy.

The Ball State 500-Yard Water Run Test (Robbins, et al., 1991) can be done lengthwise in a pool of constant depth, or it can be done widthwise across the shallow end of a pool of variable depth. A good plan is to have participants work in pairs; one partner is on deck counting completed laps for the other runner. For the most accurate results, runners should carve their own paths through the water and should avoid drafting in the wake of another runner. Runners should use their arms to pull as they run, but they must remain in a vertical body position. No swimming is allowed. Feet should touch the bottom on each step.

GOAL   The goal is to run 500 yards in the water as quickly as possible.

DIRECTIONS

1. Measure the pool and calculate the number of lengths or widths required to cover 500 yards.

...continued

Adapted from S. Grosse, 2001, "Ball State water run test: High school norms," *Journal of ICHPER-SD 37*(1): 11-14.

FITNESS TESTING ...continued

2. Set up participants with a runner in the water and a partner on deck to count laps.
3. Use a stopwatch to keep the time.
4. Runners should warm up with a couple minutes of easy jogging in the water.
5. To give runners of different heights a similar level of water resistance in a variable-depth pool, each runner should select a starting point along the pool wall where the water level is at a midpoint between his navel and nipple line. Start shorter runners in shallower water, taller runners in deeper water.
6. Runners position in the water. On a starting signal, they run the necessary number of widths. Record the running time to the nearest second.
7. Runners should cool down and stretch after the run.
8. Check the following tables to determine fitness level.

Norms for the Ball State Water Run are available in several categories. Original norms provide comparison data for individuals age 18 to 30 (Robbins, et al., 1991). Norms for high school students age 14 to 18 are also available (Grosse, et al., 2001). The original norms are based on a population of individuals of variable swimming ability. High school norms are available for a population of all ability levels, with separate norms adjusted for deep-water swimmers only (included here).

500-Yard Water Run Norms (Ages 18-30)	Men	Women
Excellent	<6:47	<7:56
Good	6:48-7:26	7:57-8:37
Average	7:27-8:05	8:39-9:18
Poor	8:06-8:44	9:19-9:59
Very Poor	>8:45	>10:00

500-Yard Water Run Norms (Ages 14-18 Deep)	
Excellent	<6:35
Good	6:36-7:11
Average	7:12-7:55
Poor	7:56-8:42
Very Poor	>8:41

HOLIDAY CELEBRATIONS

Are your lifeguards distracted during the week before a major holiday? Toward the end of the summer season, do you often hear "I won't be here then; college is starting"? How much does your staff attendance differ during various times of the year? Can you count on your lifeguards making your program a priority in their lives when other special events are prominent? If your answers to these questions show absence patterns that you would rather not have, then perhaps you need to do a bit more celebrating. Everyone loves a celebration. Make holiday time at the pool something your lifeguard staff won't want to miss. Celebrate those holidays!

The holidays are coming. You, personally, can't wait. Special dinners are planned. Gatherings with friends are on the calendar. You've been shopping for new clothes. Now, if you could just finish work! Your professional brain is gearing down in anticipation of relaxation. Although this scenario may be great for you, how does it affect your lifeguard program? Have you ever heard anyone say "The holidays are coming—I have to gear up my program at work"? Gearing up may not be the usual option, but it is just what you need to do to make holiday times important ones for your lifeguard staff. Going to the pool is a popular recreational option for other people's holiday leisure time. Your lifeguards need to get into the holiday spirit and be ready to join the celebration.

WHY GEAR UP FOR THE HOLIDAYS? Everyone is busy, very busy! Holidays increase the load, and low-priority events get crossed off the calendar. Work missed before or during a holiday season may be the beginning of an employment precedent—"call in sick when busy." Worse, some other seasonal job may replace employment in your aquatic program. Major winter holidays usually include a plethora of party opportunities. During summer holidays, the out-of-doors beckons. Spring has spring break, and fall has a back-to-school rush. It's easy to find other important things to do just within the scope of daily life. Like it or not, other activities compete for the attention of your lifeguards, and, yes, recovery from some of those events also takes away from time on the job.

Employee retention is also affected by program variety. "I don't need to be there. They'll make do or get a sub. Nothing ever happens at our pool, anyhow." The same old thing generates the same old iffy response to attendance. Your employees' once important new job as a lifeguard slips into boring repetition without you even realizing it. What generates your comfort, in terms of ease of implementation, also generates boredom and sameness for your lifeguards. Bored employees will look elsewhere.

Good job habits should be a lifelong part of a person's lifestyle. People's lives include holidays. Encouraging lifeguards to maintain their job responsibilities through a holiday period helps ensure that staffing patterns remain stable. Increasingly, aquatic managers must take steps to make sure their employees' dedication to the job (and training) can compete successfully with holiday events. Otherwise, employers will see fluctuations in staffing and will end up riding that staff shortage roller coaster.

...continued

Adapted from S. Grosse, 2005, "Happy holidays, P.S. don't forget to celebrate!" *AKWA 19*(2): 9-11.

PLANNING YOUR CELEBRATION   Here are six ways you can add celebration to your program:

- Add music.
- Vary activities.
- Add color.
- Use props.
- Introduce food.
- Adjust scheduling or privileges.

Add Music

Some holidays are closely associated with music—from the jingle of Christmas through Celtic St. Pat's to the patriotic marches of the Fourth of July and the spooky sounds of Halloween. Add music to pool sessions and celebrate. Background music playing during an open swim or as a class comes into the pool can set a festive mood. Add underwater speakers, and lap swimming rocks to a beat. Make water exercise to music a part of a special conditioning workout. Caution: The on-duty lifeguard should not be responsible for running the sound system. This is not an aspect of patron surveillance. Put a stack of CDs into the player before patrons enter and just let them play. Or you can tune in to a radio music station.

Vary Activities

Just as each holiday has its own music, many holidays also have movements associated with them. Blend those movements into conditioning activities. When the background of a participant is known, add a folk dance to help celebrate that person's birthday, anniversary, or marriage. Three-count variations of waltz music can help set the mood for Valentine's Day. Square dance movements can welcome spring (to celebrate the finish of garden planting), summer (with the first ear of corn on the cob), or fall (to celebrate harvest). The Easter bunny hop, summer rope skipping, sneaky Halloween character movements, and the spinning of the Hanukkah dreidel can all be used.

Add Color

Your staff's swimsuits, T-shirts, headbands or hats, and shoelaces can all change color with the holidays. Even a program with specific guard attire can add ribbons and poster decorations. Announce your holiday celebrations ahead of time, and encourage participants to dress for the occasion. Most individuals will not have several swimsuits, but a special hair band or cap can color any celebration. Your pool water can also be dressed for the occasion. Well, maybe not the whole pool. But, you can freeze large blocks of ice in the color of the season. For participants who claim you put ice cubes into the pool, adding a block of green ice before their St. Patrick's Day class can prove them right. A block of deep blue ice can help cool them off on a warm summer day. The ice won't last long, but the fun will. Food coloring won't harm your pool chemistry.

Use Props

Holidays and special events have props. Uncle Sam's hat for Presidents' Day, a broom for spring cleaning, a baseball cap for the opening of the season, a Pilgrim hat for Thanksgiving, and of course the Santa hat for Christmas would all provide an extra touch. Is it difficult to guard with props? Sometimes. That tall hat might have to sit behind the lifeguard on the deck or hang on a wall hook. Don't overlook decoration of bulletin boards and notice areas. Be sure to spruce up your locker rooms.

Introduce Food

Holidays are usually associated with food, not necessarily heart-healthy food, but food nonetheless. If your program already includes a healthy snack after a training session, vary this snack to recognize the holiday and still maintain a heart-healthy theme. If you do not include food in your program, special events might be a good time to add a food snack, creating a party atmosphere. Staff won't want to miss a day with special treats. Even a special treat in the staff break room says, "We think you are special." Heart-healthy muffins, fruit the color of the season, and a special heart-healthy dessert are all reasons not to miss a work session right before a holiday.

Adjust Scheduling or Privileges

Routines change during holiday times. In addition to adding holiday-specific sessions, consider allowing guards to bring a guest to the sessions they are working. Reinforce responsible guard behavior—that is, attending to the job, not the guest. If it's a training session, allow a guest to watch the training or, if appropriate, be a victim. You may recruit a new guard trainee. Holidays often mean that people have company from out of town. Rather than have lifeguards miss work to entertain, allow one or two guest privileges to be used anytime. Then a guest (in town for a birthday, confirmation, graduation, and so on) can visit at any time. Although taking a guest to work is not something that is appropriate in the adult workplace, staying away from work to entertain a guest isn't appropriate either. Your teens are still developing their work habits. Meeting them halfway on the guest question can keep them at your program, where your long-term influence can have a greater effect.

Don't Just Cancel—Reschedule!

The Wednesday before Thanksgiving is traditionally a difficult scheduling day, the day after Christmas is the best day to shop—this list could go on and on. If the pool will be open and classes or open swims in session, that's great. If not (e.g., when Christmas and New Year's Day fall on a Tuesday), you should avoid cancellation or staging a training term with fewer sessions. Instead, reschedule by providing a session on another day and time. Will everyone be able to make it? Probably not. But, you can add the altered arrangements into the registration information so that people know ahead of time. You are making an effort. If the pool schedule is full, consider pool sharing or a combined activity just for this special circumstance. Using a section of the pool during open swim is

...continued

a bit of a disruption, but it is also advertisement for your program. Continuing a schedule reinforces that "work does go on" and encourages lifeguards to blend their work and social schedules with flexibility.

WHICH HOLIDAYS?   At Disneyland, every day is a holiday. You might not want to go that far, but the holidays you celebrate are limited only by your imagination. Avoid holidays that might be offensive to your specific participant population (e.g., at a Jewish community center, it might not be a good idea to celebrate Christmas), but celebrate everything else (see table 7.3).

Table 7.3 Holiday Celebrations

Season	Major holiday	Minor holiday	General event
Spring	St. Patrick's Day Easter Mother's Day	Mardi Gras May Day Prom First day of spring Memorial Day	Spring cleaning Spring training Opening day for baseball Snow melt
Summer	Father's Day Fourth of July	First day of summer State or county fair	Opening of an outdoor movie Camping
Fall	Halloween Thanksgiving	First day of fall Labor Day Homecoming	Back to school Harvest Leaf raking and yard cleanup
Winter	Hanukkah Kwanzaa Christmas New Year's Day	First day of winter Presidents' Day Valentine's Day	Jack Frost or first snow Snow shoveling Basketball season
Anytime	Birthday Anniversary	Graduation Report card grades	Moving away New employees Awareness events (e.g., breast cancer or heart disease) Local celebrations Charitable causes

PLANNING   A celebration is what you make it. Whether a simple greeting, one piece of holiday music, a single holiday decoration, or a complete holiday-themed session, recognition of holidays can promote your program. However, just as holiday celebrations at home take planning, so do holiday observances at your pool. Start with your program calendar. Mark your training sessions, certification updates, preservice or prehiring testing, and other events that take place on specific dates. Then look for closely adjacent holidays. Begin your holiday celebration plan there. Table 7.4 shows a sample schedule for spring events.

Once your chart is completed, keep it with your calendar. Each week, check to see which events are coming up next. Keep a few additional activities in mind for those quick announcements by lifeguards—such as "Today is my birthday"—and be ready to add them in at the last moment.

Table 7.4 Holiday Planning

Holiday	Music	Movement	Color	Props	Food	Information	Schedule
St. Patrick's Day Tuesday, March 17	Traditional: Irish Washerwoman; Chieftains; Gaelic Storm; Celtic for relaxation	Jigs and reels; highland fling steps; Celtic relaxation	Green	Top hat; shamrock	Green juice	Nutrition, green foods	No changes
Easter Sunday, April 6	Bunny hop; *Easter Parade*	Bunny and chick; egg hunt	Yellow	Easter basket	Hard-boiled, decorated eggs	Recipe for tofu chocolate brownies (and samples)	Allow Good Friday staff members to reschedule.
Prom Saturday, May 8	Teen dance music	Popular teen dances	Pastels	Flowers	Cookies	Safe partying	Everyone gets an extra 10 minutes in the shower.

CELEBRATE! "There's always something new happening." "We always have so much FUN!" "I wouldn't miss THAT." These statements should be what your guards are saying about your aquatic program. Make holiday times special times when everyone just has to be at work in your pool. Plan to celebrate and have FUN!

JOURNALING

JOURNALING

Encourage lifeguards to keep journals. Progress in developing physical conditioning is easier to recognize when timed drill results and fitness testing scores are compared over time. By listing the skills they have learned, participants are creating a visual representation of accomplishment. This is particularly useful when participants must keep track of all skills in order to plan for challenge practice. Expressing attitudes, feelings, and emotions on paper provides an important release of tension, as well as a means of later analyzing how these intangibles came into being and what is being done about them.

Narrative writing of the type done in journaling is also important for documentation of accident and unusual incident situations. Although this type of documentation should be opinion free, having experience writing coherent sentences, logical paragraphs, and appropriate sequences is important to any documentation process.

A typical journal entry includes the date of writing and a brief statement of topic. Writing can be stimulated by questions. These should be open-ended questions (not yes or no questions). Here are some examples of effective questions:

- What is the most difficult skill for you to do? What are you doing to make this skill easier?
- What is the easiest skill for you to perform? Why do you think this skill is easy for you?
- What are your goals for improving your physical condition? How do you think you can reach these goals?
- What is the most frightening thing about being a lifeguard? What are you doing to reduce this fear?
- What is the most important job of a lifeguard? How can you prepare to do that job?
- What have you done this week (or month, session, and so on) to be a good role model for younger aquatic participants?
- How do you see your role as a member of this lifeguard team (training group, facility staff, and so on)? Are you a leader or follower, a strong or weak swimmer, a helper or hinderer?
- What qualities make a good lifeguard? Which of these qualities do you already have? Which ones do you think you still need to develop?
- What is the best thing about working in this program (or at this pool, with this team, and so on)?
- What would you change about this job (or program, facility, and so on) if you could?

Ponderisms can also be a part of journaling. A ponderism provides excellent journaling material. Ponderisms are those quotable quotes that make us reflect on higher values in life. They remind us of ethics, and they reaffirm our beliefs. Providing a ponderism for individuals in leadership training presents a rich table from which an expanding mind can feast. Ponderisms can be found in a variety of literature sources. Here are just a few samples:

Experience is a hard teacher. She tests first and teaches afterward.

—Schmidt, T., *Bright Spot: The Quotable Cat.* Philadelphia, PA: Running Press, 1992.

If you could identify one thing destiny probably held in store for you, what would you say it is?

—McFarlane, E., & Saywell, J., If . . .. New York: Villard, 1996.

Whether you think you can or think you can't—you are right.

—Henry Ford, *Teacher's Inspirations.* Lombard, IL: Great Quotations, 1990.

Do not follow where the path may lead . . . Go instead where there is no path and leave a trail.

—Unknown

To conquer fear is the beginning of wisdom.

—Larranaga, R., *Heart and Soul of Leadership.* Bloomington, MN: Garborg's Heart 'n Home, Inc., 1993, February.

Encourage lifeguards to read what they write in their journals. They should not just read the entry as they write it; the writers should wait a day, a week, a month, or even a year and then go back and read the entries again. Writers learn to write by writing. Although your lifeguards most likely won't be professional writers, within the sphere of emergency response and rescue, they should be thinkers. What better way to think than reading something they wrote as they were going through the growth and development process of becoming a competent lifeguard?

JUNIOR GUARD ACTIVITIES

An additional challenge faced by every aquatic manager is ensuring a continual flow of incoming staff. Turnover in lifeguard employment is a fact of life in aquatics. What can aquatic managers do to help make sure a sufficient quantity of future lifeguards are available to meet staffing needs? The best strategy is to implement a junior lifeguard program.

Each program director must decide on an entry-level age for participants. Ideally, a swimmer should be able to spend from one to three full years in a junior guard program. During that time, the swimmer should move through a hierarchy of activities to progressively develop the knowledge and skills appropriate for entry into formal lifeguard training. Although junior guard programs should be inclusive—providing opportunities for anyone qualified and interested in participation—any young person must become a strong swimmer before entry into any aquatic leadership program. Leadership training is not a substitute for learning to swim well.

Summarizing Fawcett (2001), a firm foundation in basic aquatic skills is fundamental . . . early focus on stroke correction, swimming endurance, and other basic skills will increase their confidence and better prepare them for eventual entry into the lifeguard training program. This means learning to swim must come first. Youth aspiring to enter a junior guard program should be able to demonstrate mastery of the front crawl, back crawl, breaststroke, side stroke, and elementary backstroke. Young swimmers should also have endurance using a variety of strokes, demonstrated by at least a five- to eight-minute continuous, multistroke swim. Young swimmers should also demonstrate comfort in surface diving and underwater swimming. This includes working underwater without goggles or a face mask. Lastly, the ability to tread water for several minutes is critical.

Are competitive swimmers good candidates for junior guard training? On first glance, they may seem so. However, many competitive swimmers specialize in one or two strokes. They can swim fast on the surface while wearing goggles. However, these swimmers may not have a wide range of strokes in their repertoire. They are also unlikely to have skills in below-surface swimming, and they may be unable to function without goggles. Their skills in treading water may also be underdeveloped. This does not mean that competitive swimmers should not enter a junior guard program. It does mean that they should round out their aquatic skills first by participating in swim lessons and working their way up to the junior guard program.

A sound junior guard program has several characteristics. Youth do not become lifeguards by just hanging around and being pool rats. Youth become junior guards (and later lifeguards) through a structured system of activities. An effective junior guard program includes the following:

- Entry-level criteria, including swim skills as well as age and behavioral characteristics
- A job description defining what the participant is (a junior guard), as well as what the participant is not (a lifeguard)
- A list of tasks appropriate for that job description, including levels of performance that demonstrate growth in the program

- A variety of program levels through which a participant can progress
- Job training, including specific training to accomplish the tasks in the job description
- Performance evaluations that occur on a regular basis to confirm growth in the program, as well as to remediate problems
- Ongoing supervision by an appropriate role model
- Opportunities to demonstrate leadership abilities
- Peer group bonding activities (fun and social in nature) to facilitate group cohesiveness
- An overriding focus on aquatic safety
- Apparel and badges appropriate to the junior guard group that should be worn when participating in activities of the group

Junior guard development also involves selecting appropriate tasks for training future aquatic leaders. Tasks can be modified to accommodate various age and maturity levels. Task supervisors can provide guidance necessary for leadership growth. Leadership development programs can have multiple layers, providing something for every age and developmental level. Content for junior guard programs can be drawn from a variety of sources, depending on local program characteristics, equipment availability, national-level programs already in place, and experience and expertise of program leaders (see table 7.5).

Junior lifeguard groups are typically made up of strong swimmers who are not yet old enough to take national-level lifeguard training. The age range is from about age 9 or 10 through age 14. Several national organizations provide programs to support this type of implementation. These programs include the American Red Cross Guard Start, Jeff Ellis and Associates Junior Lifeguard program, and the United States Lifesaving Association's Junior Lifeguard program. For more information, see Resources on page 233.

Appropriate tasks for youth in junior lifeguard programs include the following:

- Performing facility cleanup, putting away equipment, organizing equipment storage, and doing minor equipment repair
- Performing preliminary safety checks of the facility
- Performing preliminary water testing
- Giving orientation on pool rules to individuals their own age or younger
- Planning or leading an aquatic activity for younger groups during an open swim
- Being a victim for lifeguard practice of backboarding or first aid skills
- Being an unresponsive victim for rescue practice
- Teaching safety skills to younger participants
- Assisting with staging special pool events
- Attending lifeguard meetings as an observer

...continued

Table 7.5 Junior Guard Content

General content area	Specific skills	Associated knowledge area
Personal safety	Basic swim skills—five major strokes, deep-water swimming, treading water, entries and exits	Selection of time and place for personal swimming Rules for safe swimming Buddy systems Decision making related to behavior and peer pressure
Self-rescue	Swimming with clothes on Disrobing Release of cramp Survival float Use of personal flotation device	Application of learned skills in this category
Small craft safety	Handling craft on land Boarding and disembarking Propulsion of craft Capsize Safe resting position and injury check Swamped return to shore Craft shakeout (deep water or shallow)	Selection of time and place for small craft activities Selection of craft Sizing of equipment Weight limits and craft trimming Weather Setting up a camp (at waterfront)
Records and reports	Writing accurate descriptions of events Documenting statistics Maintaining class records	Fact versus opinion writing Pool record keeping
Providing for safety of others	Performing facility safety check Facility cleanup, including decontamination Hazard assessment Communication with younger patrons	Liability and risk management Contagion risks Pool rules and rule enforcement Setting up a safe backyard pool
First aid	CPR First aid	Responding to emergencies CPR and first aid content at the appropriate level (with certification if appropriate) Wilderness first aid or first aid in situations where help may be delayed (if appropriate to setting)
Rescue of others	Reaching rescue with arm, leg, or towel Reaching rescue with rescue tube Reaching rescue with pole Throwing rescue with ring buoy or throw rope bag Wading rescue with equipment Surface diving and underwater swimming Use of mask, fins, and snorkel	Selection of rescue method Calling for assistance Search and underwater retrieval of objects Application of skills to skin diving and scuba

General content area	Specific skills	Associated knowledge area
Employment	Job application completion Employment interviewing Preemployment screening for skills Activities requiring functioning as a member of a team Role playing handling difficult personal interactions related to employment	Job seeking Employment application and interview process Personal job record (on time, work ethics, absence) Teamwork on the job Certification and recertification process Chain of command Job evaluation process
Ancillary aquatic skills	Any aquatic skill not already developed by participant (up to swimming rescues)	Venues for participation Equipment Program availability for specific aquatic activity

The following tasks are inappropriate for youth in junior lifeguard programs:

- Substituting for a lifeguard (even in shallow water)
- Performing safety or water checks in place of those done by certified staff
- Performing facility cleanup of hazardous or blood-borne pathogen materials
- Mixing or handling pool chemicals
- Being a responsive drowning victim for rescue practice
- Completing legal records and reports
- Participating in any confidential conferences or meetings of the guard staff

The most important factor to remember when formulating job descriptions for junior guard programs is that the participants are *in training*. Participants are not trained. The purpose of the junior guard program is to develop youth for future lifeguard certification and employment. Keep expectations and assignments within the parameters of learning for future job performance, rather than for performance of an existing job.

How do you evaluate participants' performance in a junior guard program? Responsible behavior does have characteristics. Here are some questions to ask in formulating an assessment checklist for junior guards:

- What percentage of time is the participant on time for program activities?
- What percentage of time is the participant dressed appropriately for participation?
- Have you seen or heard the participant using inappropriate behavior or language? If so, how many times?
- How does the participant respond to the leadership of others?
- Can the participant take direction?

...continued

- Can the participant work as a member of a team? Have you seen this demonstrated? In what way?
- Does the participant volunteer for extra or unpleasant tasks?
- How does the participant handle providing direction to others? Have you seen this demonstrated? In what way?
- Is the participant interested in improving his own skills? Have you observed skill practice?
- Is the participant truthful? If you have determined untruthful behavior, how and why did it occur?
- Is the participant receptive to suggestions for improvement when negative circumstances occur? Do the negative circumstances repeat?
- Does the participant function within his job description? If not, whose job is he trying to perform?

These are specific questions that should result in answers reflecting the participants' observable behavior. Participants cannot improve what they do not acknowledge or understand. Discussing attitude has no purpose. Attitude, positive or negative, is manifested in actual behavior. Focus on the behavior. Perform evaluations quarterly (at the very least), and include information on how improvements will be assessed. Document the results.

Behavior of teenagers can be inconsistent. As with all human behavior, leadership skills may vary from day to day, situation to situation, person to person. Develop your junior guards by helping these young people make the difficult transition from child to adult—and from aquatic participant to lifeguard. Begin with swim skills and personal water safety. Extend training to include assisting others through appropriate emergency responses up to but *not* including swimming rescues. Provide opportunities for active involvement with all aspects of the safe operation of your aquatic program. Remember, from the very first day a young swimmer is at your facility, that swimmer is in aquatic leadership training.

LIFEGUARD COMPETITIONS

Lifeguard competitions provide opportunities for guards to demonstrate knowledge and skills in comparison with other guards. Almost any activity or game can be turned into a competitive event by stipulating performance criteria. Events can be any of the following:

- Performance for time
- Performance for distance
- Swim and retrieve (based on time or distance)
- Swim and tow (based on time or distance)
- Swim and perform a task (based on time, distance, or accuracy)
- Swim and perform a rescue (based on time, distance, or accuracy of technique)
- Perform a team task or rescue (based on time, distance, or accuracy)
- Rescue equipment throw (based on distance or accuracy)
- Craft propulsion (based on time, distance, or maneuverability)
- Craft rescue (based on time, distance, or accuracy of technique)
- Search and rescue (based on time or accuracy)
- Scenario (subjective decision making)

Judging time or distance is fairly easy. Judging accuracy of performance requires a knowledgeable person to evaluate performances of participants. Using a score sheet with all required actions noted allows the judge to check off each requirement as it is performed. Points can be awarded for quality of performances. Times can then be adjusted based on accuracy of performances. Additional resources on lifeguard competitions can be found in the resource list on page 233.

POLKA JOG

Roll out the barrel.
We'll have a barrel of fun.
Zing, boom, te re rah.
We've got the blues on the run . . .

Yes, it's the "Beer Barrel Polka." It may be old and a bit hokey, but it really inspires people to *move*! Better yet, that polka and others like it inspire participants to continuous movement. Turn your pool into a running track. Put on a polka CD, provide just a bit of organization, and your guards will get the workout of their lives.

SAFETY AND ORGANIZATION Polka Jog can be a shallow-water activity, a deep-water activity, or an activity moving back and forth between shallow and deep. The activity can be arranged to use whatever space is available in the pool. Participants can polka jog with no additional equipment or with equipment used to enhance the workout.

Any pool can become a running track. Line up participants along one wall. Have everyone make a quarter turn toward one end. This places them in a line, one behind the other. Then ask the person at the front of the line to start jogging slowly, following the wall of the pool. Everyone else should just follow the leader.

The group begins jogging around the perimeter of the pool (or a marked space), following the pool walls. For the first lap around, everyone should stay in line. This will help with spacing and will set the group up for safe passing. After the first lap, swimmers should be allowed to set their own pace. Advise slower joggers to stay close to the pool wall. Encourage faster joggers to pass

Adapted from S. Grosse, 2002, "Polka jog: An easy, active workout," *AKWA* 16(4): 6-8.

on the inside. Caution: This is different from running track etiquette. Passing on the inside allows slower joggers (who are perhaps more tired or less able) to remain closer to the safety of the wall.

DEEP WATER   In a pool with variable depths, the line of joggers will—all too soon—jog to the drop-off point. Positioning yourself at the drop-off will allow you to give additional advice and encouragement. Joggers should just jog right off the bottom and continue the jog without their feet actually touching anything. It becomes more of a travel tread. Remind joggers to keep their trunks vertical, rather than tipped forward into a swim position. The arms should be used for balance and should move in the same oppositional pattern used for running. Cupping the fingers will provide an assistive pull, as will wearing aqua gloves. When shallow water is reached again, joggers should allow their feet to touch bottom and should continue the more normal jogging pattern. Moving between shallow and deep water should be as flowing as possible. Caution joggers to avoid stopping, because other joggers will be coming up from the rear.

To make deep-water jogging more difficult, ask participants to put hands on hips, shoulders, or top of head. Obviously, removing hands from the activity increases the need for a strong leg kick. Difficulty may also be increased by having joggers push a buoyant object as they jog. Holding a kickboard out in front (with the narrow edge parallel to the pool bottom and the flat surface pushing water) increases resistance during the deep-water portion of the jog. When joggers reach shallow water, the held object can be used for supplementary arm exercises, such as above-the-head push-ups, while continuing to jog.

MUSIC   This is a Polka Jog. No matter how old the polka concept, the music remains a fantastic motivator of movement. Polkas don't stop! At times, they can be silly. No one can listen without at least tapping his toe, and once in a pool, that toe tapping can become a wild, creative movement experience. When jogging in shallow water, joggers can add arm actions of their own choosing. Participants can create their own or play follow the leader. A CD of polka music can play for the entire workout time; the objective is simply to continue to jog.

Does it have to be polka music? No. However, some types of music are better than others for establishing a pace and providing inspiration for a longer span of continual activity. Here are some other types of music that are appropriate for an aqua jog workout:

- Marches, particularly patriotic march music
- Irish jigs and reels
- Broadway show tunes
- Disney tunes
- Collegiate fight songs
- Square dance or line dance music

Don't forget, specific age groups have definitive music tastes. Heavy metal music, rap, rock and roll, and other teen-specific favorites at the time will motivate participants. Because people will be listening to the same type of music for

...continued

the entire jog, avoid collections having extreme and inappropriate language. For everyone to enjoy the jog, the music should be something most people will, if not enjoy, at least find tolerable for the whole time period.

DIFFICULTY   The turbulence created by the joggers can be used to increase the difficulty. With all polka joggers moving in the same direction, a current in that direction will be generated. Use a whistle sound (one that can be heard over the music) to signal a reverse of the jog direction (from clockwise to counterclockwise). This forces everyone to now move against the current. Before too long, the current itself will reverse, and jogging will be easier again. Watch the group and plan reverses for different pool positions so that participants will experience shallow-water reverses as well as deep-water reverses.

Direction of travel can also affect difficulty. Jogging forward is easiest. Try having participants jog backward (this is different from a reverse in that participants have their backs to the direction of travel). The current will offer resistance, but joggers will be using a different group of muscles. Eventually, this current will also reverse. Quick changes in direction of travel will increase difficulty; each change will be made against the current, and the speed required will encourage mental as well as physical activity.

Adding turns and spins to forward or backward travel also increases the difficulty. Turning in a circle while jogging forward is a more difficult locomotor pattern and generates more complex turbulence.

When making any changes, cue the change without stopping the jogging. Remind participants to look for you when they hear a whistle (or when you lower the music volume). After the whistle, you should quickly cue the desired change using very large arm gestures as well as vocal instructions.

LENGTH OF THE POLKA JOG SESSION   The age and general physical condition of participants should dictate the duration of a jogging session. Also consider the amount of effort that each jogger must expend participating. High school students who are also lifeguards can polka jog for 45 minutes to an hour without any flotation support and receive a great workout. Lifeguard trainees may not be in equally good physical condition. It is always easier to start with less and have everyone leave comfortable and wanting more. Be careful not to start with too much—this can happen if you underestimate the cumulative effect of the activity (especially if using additional resistance equipment or doing a jog totally in deep water). Starting with too much will leave participants not wanting to polka jog ever again.

One way to judge intensity is by asking participants to assess their perceived exertion level on a scale of 1 to 10. How hard is each person working? A rating of 1 means very little exertion is taking place. A 10 means the person is working as hard as she possibly can. How tired does the person feel? A rating of 1 means not tired at all. A 10 means extremely tired and ready to quit.

Another means of assessing exertion is the talk test. Can participants talk while jogging? In this case, talking while jogging will increase the difficulty level—so let your swimmers converse at will! If they cannot talk, they are probably overexerting themselves, and it is time to cool down and rest.

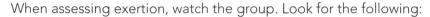

When assessing exertion, watch the group. Look for the following:

- Facial expressions. Are people smiling with the fun or grimacing from overexertion and pain?
- Skin color. Is skin color normal with good oxygenation, or are participants pink from overexertion?
- Participation pace. Are joggers moving at an even, steady pace? Or did they start out fast and fade quickly, again from overexertion? (A discussion of pace may be necessary for some participants to understand the concept.)
- Position in the pool. Everyone should be jogging. Are people hanging onto the side of the pool instead?

Polka jogging also lends itself well to heart rate monitoring. Participants can continue to jog while taking their own pulse. Accurately counting the pulse will give participants practice on a valuable CPR skill. By practicing heart rate monitoring, participants will also learn a means of maintaining fitness that they can apply during land exercise. If participants need to increase intensity to raise their heart rate, they can add a more vigorous arm action. Totally removing the arms from the activity (if a person is able to do that and still stay up and vertical) also increases the difficulty. Arms not in use can be crossed across the chest, held at water level with fingers up out of the water, or raised overhead (now, that's a *tough* way to jog!).

How do you keep track of everyone? The easiest way to keep close watch of the entire group is to walk around the pool in the direction opposite to the direction of jog travel. That way, each jogger will pass you face to face. You can wave, smile, nod encouragement, pantomime arm actions, or provide directions. Making direct eye contact provides an opportunity to assess participant comfort with the activity.

FINISHING TOUCH   Don't forget to have a cool-down. The gentle jog at the start is a good warm-up. After vigorous jogging, participants will need a few minutes of gentle stretching, relaxation, and easy breathing. Be sure to compliment all on keeping the pace.

Polka Jog is a fun activity. If your joggers have enjoyed themselves, that means they did it safely and had a good workout.

RELAYS

Relays are group events that involve each individual in a group performing a task in order for the group to complete its challenge. The smaller the individual group or relay team, the more activity each member will have. The larger the relay team, the longer each person will need to wait for his turn. Typical relay events include the following:

- Passing objects
- Carrying objects
- Traversing a distance
- Performing a task

Here are some typical relay formations and sample activities:

- Single line. Participants pass a brick down a line of people and back to the start.
- Single line with a change of position. Participants pass a brick down a line of people; when the brick is in the hands of the last person in line, that person swims and carries the brick to the head of the line and then begins the pass again.
- Single line with a traverse of a distance. A swimmer starts at the head of the line, swims to a predetermined point, touches the mark, and swims back to tag the next person in line. As the next person begins to swim, the first swimmer goes to the end of the line.
- Double-line shuttle. The relay team is divided in half, and each half is in a single-file line. The two lines are at opposite ends of the pool. The first person at the head of one line begins by swimming across to the first person in the opposite line. Once there, she passes an object or tags that individual, who now goes across to where the first swimmer started. The first swimmer goes to the rear of the line that she swam to. The second swimmer passes to or tags the person she meets at the head of the opposite line. In effect, when each person has had one turn, the two lines will have exchanged places. The relay can be doubled by allowing each person a second turn. This will return the lines to their original positions.
- Pursuit. Relay team members are stationed equidistant from each other around the swim area. The last swimmer in line begins the swim carrying an object. This swimmer swims to the participant ahead of her and passes the object to that swimmer. As soon as the second swimmer has the object in hand, she swims to the third swimmer and passes the object. This continues until the last person to receive the object swims it back to the start.

Many lifeguarding activities and games can be performed as relays. This is particularly useful when working with large groups of participants. Relays are also useful for developing team spirit.

TIMED EVENTS

Many activities and games are suitable for execution against time. A time criterion provides not only a stimulus to respond quickly, but also an objective measure of just how quickly that response occurs. Some national certification programs include timed events as part of credentialing criteria. Including timed activities in your training helps lifeguards adjust to the process of performance against the clock.

Before implementing any timed activity, be sure all participants can perform the required skills in an appropriate manner. Timing focuses on speed of performance. Increasing speed can decrease the quality of the response and can increase errors. Errors can result in injuries. Knowledge and skills required in an activity should be learned first—and then timed.

A stopwatch is the best timing device. However, timing a performance can be as easy as counting seconds. Here are some typical formats and sample activities for implementing timing:

- Timing how quickly a single task or multiple tasks can be accomplished. How quickly can a lifeguard perform 10 Brick-Ups?

- Comparing a single performance with another, subsequent, performance. How quickly can a lifeguard perform 10 Brick-Ups at the start of the season in comparison to how quickly the same lifeguard can perform 10 Brick-Ups after four weeks on the job?

- Assisting a lifeguard in assessing his performance level. Asking the lifeguard, "How many Brick-Ups do you think you can do in one minute?" or "How long do you think it will take you to perform 10 Brick-Ups?"

- Making evaluative performance comparisons among a group of lifeguards. Who can perform the most Brick-Ups in one minute?

- Providing a standard to which lifeguards can aspire. The pool record for number of Brick-Ups in one minute is 57.

Not all activities should be timed. Just as variety in training activities is essential for optimal development of conditioning and skills, so is variety in training formats. Timing is not appropriate for some lifeguard skills. Spinal injury rescue techniques, for example, require careful actions, rather than quick actions. Do not send your lifeguards mixed messages by timing rescue techniques that require slow and careful execution.

Appendix

Product Suppliers

This appendix lists commercial suppliers of lifeguarding equipment.

Aquafit Bars

Aquatics IS, Inc.
706 W. Highland Ave.
Downington, PA 19335
Joanne@aquaticsis.com
www.aquafitgear.com

First Aid
and CPR Simulation and Training Manikins

Armstrong Medical
575 Knightsbridge Pkway.
P.O. Box 700
Lincolnshire, IL 60069-0700
800-323-4220
www.armstrongmedical.com

Music

Educational Activities, Inc.
P.O. Box 392
Freeport, NY 11520
800-645-3739

Wagon Wheel Records and Books
16812 Pembrook Lane
Huntington Beach, CA 02649
714-846-8169
www.wagonwheelrecords.com

Rescue Equipment

Kiefer
1700 Kiefer Dr.
Zion, IL 60099
800-323-4071
www.kiefer.com

Scoop Ball, Spin Jammer, and Poly Equipment

US Games
P.O. Box 7726
Dallas, TX 75209
800-327-0484
www.usgames.com

Submersible Manikins, Training Materials, and Pool and Open-Water Rescue Equipment

The Lifeguard Store
2018 Eagle Rd.
Normal, IL 61761
800-846-7052
www.thelifeguardstore.com

Marine Rescue Products
P.O. Box 3484
Newport, RI 02840
800-341-9500
www.marine-rescue.com
staff@marine-rescue.com

Resources

American Red Cross. (2007). *Guard start*. Boston, MA: Staywell.

Brewster, B.C. (1995). *United States Lifesaving Association manual of open water lifesaving*. Englewood Cliffs, NJ: Prentice Hall.

Chicago Park District. (n.d.). *Guide for junior lifeguard programming*. Chicago: Chicago Park District.

Dixon, H. (2005, July). Tales from the chair: Beyond the moans and groans—what lifeguards have to say about in-service training. *Parks and Recreation, 40*(7), 52-54.

Dworkin, G.M. (1994). *Lifeguard competition guidebook*. Woodbridge, VA: Lifesaving Resources.

Fawcett, P. (2001). Keeping the lifeguard pipeline full: Junior lifeguards. *Parks and Recreation, 36*(11), 36-39.

Grosse, S. (2001, February). Post Traumatic Stress Disorder: Implications for seasonal lifeguards. *Parks and Recreation, 36*(2), 60-71.

Grosse, S. (2002, April/May). Swing and promenade for heart rate high. *AKWA, 15*(6), 9-14.

Grosse, S. (2005, August/September). Happy holidays, P.S. don't forget to celebrate! *AKWA, 19*(2), 9-11.

Grosse, S., Wieser, A., & Katula, J. (2001). Ball State water run test: High school norms. *Journal of ICHPER-SD, 37*(1), 11-14.

Jackson, E. (1990). Starting young: Junior lifeguard program offers pool of talent. *Aquatics International, 2*(2), 26-29.

Kelly, D. (1994, September). Hawaiian waterman. *Personal Watercraft Illustrated*, 64-77.

Moler, C. (1990). Ironguards strut their stuff. *National Aquatics Journal, 6*(2), 3-4.

Noble, J., & Cregeen, A. (2004). *Swimming games and activities*. London: A.C. Black.

Rheker, U. (2000). *Aquafun: Games and fun for the advanced*. Oxford, UK: Meyer and Meyer Sport.

Robbins, G., & Powers, D. (1993). The Ball State 500-yard water run: A new fitness field test for non-swimming water exercisers. *Journal of ICHPER-SD, 14*(4), 9-11.

Robbins, G., Powers, D., & Burgess, S. (1991). *A wellness way of life*. Dubuque, IA: William C. Brown.

Twenge, J. (2006). *Generation me: Why today's young Americans are more confident, assertive, and entitled—and more miserable than ever before*. New York: Simon and Schuster.

About the Author

Susan J. Grosse, MS, is the president of Aquatic Consulting & Education Resource Services in Milwaukee. Grosse has more than 45 years of experience in aquatics and education and has published extensively in the areas of aquatics and exceptional education. She is also a sought-after speaker, having presented in Ireland, Egypt, Canada, and the United States.

Grosse received a 40-year pin from the American Red Cross as a volunteer instructor and instructor trainer. She also received the Mabel Lee and Honor Awards from the American Alliance for Health, Physical Education, Recreation and Dance (AAHPERD) for her contributions to the education profession. The Aquatic Therapy and Rehab Institute presented her with a Tsunami Spirit Award for her work in aquatics with people with disabilities.

Grosse has served as chair of the Aquatic Council for AAHPERD and as president of the American Association for Active Lifestyles and Fitness. She also has been a water safety instructor trainer and a lifeguarding instructor trainer for the American Red Cross. In her leisure time she enjoys swimming, canoeing, reading, and listening to music.